Blerim Burjani

Right or Left Political Parties Orientations in Western Balkan

Blerim Burjani

Right or Left Political Parties Orientations in Western Balkan

Political Parties

Dictus Publishing

Imprint
Any brand names and product names mentioned in this book are subject to trademark, brand or patent protection and are trademarks or registered trademarks of their respective holders. The use of brand names, product names, common names, trade names, product descriptions etc. even without a particular marking in this work is in no way to be construed to mean that such names may be regarded as unrestricted in respect of trademark and brand protection legislation and could thus be used by anyone.

Cover image: www.ingimage.com

Publisher:
Dictus Publishing
is a trademark of
Dodo Books Indian Ocean Ltd. and OmniScriptum S.R.L publishing group

120 High Road, East Finchley, London, N2 9ED, United Kingdom
Str. Armeneasca 28/1, office 1, Chisinau MD-2012, Republic of Moldova, Europe
Printed at: see last page
ISBN: 978-613-7-35701-9

INSTITUTI I KOSOVES PER POLITIKA ZHVILLIMORE (IKPZH)

BLERIM BURJANI

Right or Left Political Parties Orientations in Western Balkan

INSITUTI I KOSOVES PER POLITIKA ZHVILLIMORE(IKPZH)

BLERIM BURJANI

Right or Left Political Parties Orientations in Western Balkan

author
Email:burjani@yahoo.com
Number of telephone +37744502546
Pristina,2018

CONTENT:

Abbreviations

AAK-Alliance For Future of Kosovo

LDK-Democratic League of Kosovo

PDK-Democratic Parties of Kosovo

PSD-Party of Social Democracy

NISMA-Social democracy

PPK-Parliament Party of Kosovo

LPK-Popular Movement of Kosovo

UNIKOMB-National Unite

LKCK-Movement for Liberalization of Kosovo

VV-Self - Determination Movement

PTK-Post Telecom of Kosovo

PD-Democratic Party

SDP- Social Democrat Party

LSI-Socialist Movement for Integration

PS -Socialist Party

UP-University of Pristina

DPS -Democratic Party of Socialists

Democratic Alternative (DA),

Democratic Party of Albanians (DPA),

Liberal Democratic Party (LDP)

Liberal Party (LP)

Party of Democratic Prosperity (PDP)

Social Democratic Union of Macedonia (SDSM)

, Internal Macedonian Revolutionary Organization - Democratic Party for Macedonian National Unity (VMRO-DPMNE)

Introduction

Balkan states are still at a stage of political and class transformation. There is no stable market economy that would affect the strengthening of the aspect of building a party political orientations, both left and right political programs . Balkan political developments are charismatic in two matter: the first is the formation of the economic classes and the second nationalism as an ideology. Without the formation of economic classes there is no neither a proper and clear party profile. The problems of the Balkan States are characterized by major economic problems, with a greater unemployment and inefficiency and in bad developments of law and order. Balkan states have long been trying to form economic classes. The Balkan countries are more concerned with the problems of regional nationalism ,which is bad and not good for the region. While domestic political developments are not stable. In Albania strives to have Clear division but more formal than functional, on the one side there is the right path of the DP and on the other two parties left PS and LSI. While in Kosovo there is no clear division of the political class in formal way are PDK and LDK and another part is LVV,NISMA,PSD. In Serbia there are different right-wing, leftist nationalistic problems, also with the problems of stable economic classes. In Serbia, they still have power over the nationalist party and the socialist party. Macedonia is faced with the many twisted, left-wing, social-democrat and nationalist left-wing currents. Montenegro also has left-wing socialist, rightist, and nationalist leftist currents.

CHAPTER ONE

Qualification of parties in Kosovo right or left or center

1. Why the left political movements in Kosovo?

If we analyze well, we can clearly see that Publicly Owned Enterprises that have "abundant" and profitable money are being used in building social policies and to spent them in the social matter until now in Kosovo. It is beginning to be used citizens budget to reduce extreme poverty, especially that of social housing and building a better social welfare that is been seen until now and can be expected to happen in the future as well. Recent events such as the signing of a Memorandum of Understanding between the Government and PTK for the construction of homeless homes could be one of the "left" elements in Kosovo and then "ban" in the private sector development of education and the "restriction " drastically "in the name of enforcement " of Public University ", almost all non-public institutions of higher education in Kosovo had the accreditation as named " colleges ", the not-existing term in the law on private higher education in region, so dominated the Public University of Pristina, which is more "free" than the private education, this has happened during the governance of the two right parties PDK but also the reconciliation of the LDK, is the second segment that shows that the right-wing political party is dealing with the leftist politics. the right political party PDK has established public universities despite the lack of cadres in Kosovo cities such as Gjilan, Peja, Gjakova, Prizren, Mitrovica these actions were understood as counter private colleges by preventing students enrolling in expensive colleges, while public university payments are more formal. these actions were understood as opposed to private colleges by preventing students from enrolling in expensive colleges, while public university fees are very cheap. What are the other important steps for profiling the "left"? Establishment of the Unemployment Fund, the Health Fund and the Social Protection Fund and the exclusion of social categories from taxes that may be severe for life for them? Through this Social Protection Fund will increase social assistance at the expense of taxation in the country, this is understandable. Establishing the Fund for Protection and Safety at Work, which- would again charge the top business to allocate funds where the companies would try to coordinate activities with workers' unions. Then the state would impose higher taxes on private care facilities health and narrow the uncontrollable development opportunities of this sector. The strengthening of the public sector in Kosovo, the increase of salaries for civil servants, the increase of taxes and the continuous control of private capital from left to the action and registration of joint stock companies and the control of private capital, are the elements that today could be faced in social-political issues in Kosovo.

2. Are we building up the "social" state ?

Slowly and "without tremble" we are resuming the construction of a social state. So some people in Kosovo think like this. This seems to favor a part of the citizens for a "left" profile in the service of workers and social strata in Kosovo, there is no real courage to declare that they belong to the "left" profile. It is in the interest of the citizens to happen to profile. Why not? Political parties should have a profile that means "liberal", "left" or center. It's interesting if we compare Kosovo left policy with other stats in Europe and how was born in "left Europe'?. Europeans, when they were "overwhelmed by the capitalists, began to say" they have not taken care of the poor "and create better conditions for the poor population, the labor class, and the middle class, by trying to keep the" middle class " as a buffer zone between extremely poor and "big riches people ". Do Kosovar politicians want to keep Kosovo non development country and always with problems in social aspect ? In the middle-class scheme take part as a civil servant in Kosovo, second, we have the individual family business- SME business, and Publicly Owned Enterprises and small manufacturing companies while many companies that run the biggest annual business profit are completely small. What does this mean? This means that the cadre can jump on the social care of the state.

Building "left" or "right" policies by political parties are in the benefit of Kosovo's citizens. It would be best for citizens to have clear profile political parties and to build clear concepts to support the citizen with clear objectives. Until now political parties as they are without profile with "program waste of mixed profiles", and fear that they may be not to show their profile stand "left" or " the "right", saying that they could lose the support of the citizens if they show that", right and left policy ". For them, is better like this to not show preferences which they are!

3. The "left" or right?

The "left political orientations ", in Kosovo are not very popular and is not "desirable in the population". Perhaps this is not the mistake to have a such fillings , because Kosovo was leaded by communists with much poorness and with communist political violence, maybe there should not be such of this "term" for any political parties in Kosovo as example 'Socialist Party of Kosovo", until now in such political orientations is not happened in Kosovo. It is not incidental why they all left parties in Kosovo have different symbols, but not equal with old communist system. Left in Kosovo can be defined for the moment as an "attempt" to build a "social state", with fear of open and transparent program action, such as free education, free public health, and better stimulated wages. Left policy could be understood when political parties deals with real social issues and law reforms in the economy and maintaining balance in the economic development in the state. In reality, this is not happening in Kosovo. Europe has long-standing political function and has its own history of enough to show its class background and the struggle to support the labors class a much they need, the states have now built a broadly social democratic tradition in their states such are for example Norway, Finland, and Sweden. The fear of coming up with a completely clear "left" program is a particular risk of being frightened of the "righteous" people, who show "their teeth" in their search for power and their fear of being dogged right in an extreme poverty-stricken state over 15%, with about 42% of enrolled people in employment. Who knows how many people may be unemployed when there are no clear statistics until now in Kosovo. The danger lies in the fear of proclamation that we are going to have a state like Haiti, where 70% of the population is poor where the captivity system is installed or built riches, or Burma and the Dominican Republic.

4. Why should we be "right"

To be right we must be "rich", with high taxes on the poor and middle class with no all-round state funding but with voluntary funds, with the empowerment of the economy for the big companies, working for high annual profits and the with protection of poverty people , full economy of the individual business class and SMEs under the dictates of young newborn capitalists in Kosovo who will slowly grow and increase employment and will not be too bored for social balance even though they are scarce in Kosovo but a rich menu of "luxuries", the most expensive tuition and quality of faculty division of rich and poor class.

The poor in time should go to the Public University and others would go to the private education system that after a period of time would create greater and better experiences. The public health sector trend for that as it has now received in Kosovo . These would be clear symptoms that there are elements of installing "the righteous life in a blissful Kosovo", enriching the rich in continuity, poverty is decreasing as employment increases steadily as the state reduces assistance and social funds. The right-wing state will not announce enrichment limits for the moment in Kosovo and should not be stopped from enrichment, but it should consistently create relief for small companies that will be in the service of large enterprises or will be ingested by "big companies "The export growth and the strengthening of the market economy and the struggle for international markets would start to the extent necessary and the co-operation of Kosovo's major economic enterprises with those of other states. What life do the citizens of Kosovo want "Right or Left" political orientation".

Citizens see us and listen carefully to what they talk about the party's profile. It is a general impression that if you are a supporter of a "right" political orientations it is better because for many years ruling in Albania are "the right" party but no more for now is ruling the left socialist party in Albania, so there are many citizens who think and wish to build a powerful state with order and law and for the large expense in the general social sector is better, while the "righteous life" will bring gl The persistent ineffective economic developments and the forgetfulness that we used to be "different" then poor, and now the policy development to be followed is a good idea to be "righteous or bourgeois"? Most of the younger generations in Kosovo are not educated in the spirit of the right program policies, the older part of the generations have grown and developed with left-wing political programs in the communist system of Kosovo, in that system the students were freed from fees for studies in all faculties and universities then hoped to find work in the state sector or work in public companies that have high salaries or become future governors. Now it is the opposite, all of them first have to come to the stage of existence of economic life to think and to build individualized businesses with a proper entrepreneurial education, further to achieve higher education or have to perform only vocational education to work in factories or using bank loans and other forms to build individual business. So if we are doing a public opinion analysis: "Do you want to have good bourgeois programming politics" and the state to run the rich people the answer would be "YES". But the problem of how to become rich then take governance with the state? Here the answer is usually difficult in Kosovo , people are enriched with getting in illegally form and against laws in force , this time answer is "NO". People in Kosovo want to lead the state by intelligence but not those who are enriched in violation of the law or are suspected of illegal enrichment ,those are problematic only few of them have honest and those do a business with clean capital.

Because the one who has enough private capital and to grow continuously will know better how to develop the economy than those who talk about social welfare and not for enriching the economy but how to get a better support for poor population. "Intrinsic we are "Sui generics", nothing can be done "properly" even if we are still dissatisfied or when we do not know what to do it should find guilty of guardianship.

The political party life in Kosovo is sitting on the left - wings and as well in the right -wings, until we get tired, and to have the profile for political parties , there is no way without profiling political parties and to solve many problems in our society. How to be economically or rightly developed in Kosovo? A big matter issue for now still without a profiling policy. Should we first think completely different? How far have we thought so far, efforts must be made to build a sound economic education system, then we have to capitalize or increase our private wealth, we must think rather to enjoy less, but we must continue to make efforts to we have enough wealth to put in the binary of the money's rotation and the private capital that we have. To build the will for a powerful economy by building small companies up to those giant companies that emerge in the international economy and become part of the economic giants of the Balkan and Europe regions. "Right" education has been missing in Kosovo for one the whole lesson was how to survive but not how to be rich. We need to think that a right-wing state we want to have must have the fully-fledged right-of-the-way economic capital program. In large companies, those that are working by using small and medium-sized enterprises to make them dependent on the company great, we need a clear, clear economic strategy.

5. Can we build a right economy?

We need international assistance and expertise in economic transformation, but we need to know what we want to achieve in order to get the appropriate international financial assistance. Building a deeply reformed economy, giving top priority to enterprise development and the idea entrepreneurship with a system of education quite differently. This cannot be done quickly but should be started with great steps to move on economic reforms and not to stop looking back.

Why we need to be clear - "to understand others", to privatize what needs to be said or just over 90% of our "tired" economy, there is stagnation in strategy, but a new strategy for economic transformation , "Rightists" can do it. Kosovo has a strategy that has been designed and is being "shelved", this should motivate us to build a right economic strategy of a strong economic and orderly rule of law in our country. It is quite possible to try as soon as possible to get away from "social poverty" and to integrate into the European economy.

6. Kosovo and Fond Policy

 Kosovo in its social aspect does not have the funds that would enable a social and health welfare of the citizens. For better future in Kosovo, a left-handed ounce should have these funds established:

- The Fund for Sickness Insurance
- Fund for the Protection of Mother and Childe
- Family Protection Fund
- Fund for the Protection of the Elderly
- Youth Investment Fund
- Maternity Leave Fund
- The Fund for Unemployed
- Disability Fund
- Fund for Protection and Security at Work

Kosovo has no economic rush to create different social funds and effective social protections, economic and health support in adequate manner. Kosovo according to the economic development in this situation of economy can be based on three vital funds for citizens such as:

- Fund for Health Insurance
- Social Protection Fund
- Fond per Protection of Mother and Childe

Kosovo has lost its haven to being a social state, since from the UNMIK period, UNMIK mission did not allow a social state to be built, despite the great efforts of the Government of Kosovo in 2003, UNMIK rejected all proposals of local government at that time, the Ministry of Labor and Social Welfare had requested the fund for the protection of children, which was not allowed by UNMIK. In the period following the declaration of Kosovo independence since 2008, there is no debate on establishing the fund for the protection of children and mothers, so Kosovo is trying to survive in the social sense with a lot of hardship as a result of such a policy has fallen natality in Kosovo almost 35%, the lack of child care institutionally through an adequate fund has happened that poverty grows more and more and marriages take place over the age of 30. The lack of adequate institutional care natality in Kosovo is falling far enough. There are some interesting developments in Kosovo in terms of building a left-wing orientation policy in Kosovo and increasing the populist left-wing politics, a political subject "Vetvendosje" has twice succeeded in gaining power at the local level, thus winning the elections in the capital of Kosovo - Pristina, this party is oriented towards left-wing program policies. Now in Kosovo there are three parties political orientation with themes of left "Vetëvendosje", Social Democratic Party and NISMA Social-Democrats , so these parties have political statements that are left, although they have big problems building left politics because they have no personal experience and they are faced with professional   problems for making such policies that the state of social content will gradually come. There is no socialist party in Kosovo because of the heavy damages that brought Kosovo citizens to the time when Kosovo was communist, there are many criticisms and there has never been any attempt to build a classical party on the left until now in Kosovo , so today there are no such parties with this name in Kosovo.

 Kosovo is likely to have leftist politics since a large part of the political generations have praised the socialist system by calling it a state of social rights, so Kosovo had enough funds to hold education and health free of charge, education was public and free at all levels, while higher education had a formal salary that paid students, but also for this all students once had student loan support. At present, the demographic aspect of Kosovo has changed, the old communist generation is replacing by a new generation completely free to think more about a classical capitalist state. It is surprising that today in Kosovo there are three parties that are part of the Assembly of Kosovo who have a political programming left over. Communist Kosovo until 1989-90 was poor and unobtrusive, but at that time there were two social classes in the communist era, bureaucratic class consisting of the directors of numerous Communist enterprises, and state employees, doctors and professors at all levels, the engineers were the advantaged class while the greater part was about 80% of the social labors class, that communist system was ferocious that it was a poor labor-class state and with great difficulty were educated, relatively looking Kosovo was poor since the years after the Second World War which was gradually educated, but in the 1970s there was a good lifestyle in communist Kosovo for the bureaucratic class, for professors, doctors, and engineers, since the labor class had also achieved that the workers' children as class social life of that time had to be educated and become part of a bureaucratic class in that time. Socialist –communist romance in Kosovo has ended a long time. Today with other different social ideas and there are some program ideas that think Kosovo is still a poor country with big social problems with large unemployment and the disappearance of some professional profiles for job placement in western states, doctors, engineers as well as architects and people with vocational schools find work in Germany, there are a considerable number of Kosovars working in Germany and have been employed in this country. And there are ideas in Kosovo to develop a social profile even though there are criticisms of some parties of the right orientations, but not the harsh critic of the political leftist orientation, while the Democratic Party of Kosovo (PDK) is a half- left social political party because there are many people who are influential in this party that have left behind ideas, however this party in the program of its own says it is a party with program with rights orientations policy. In Kosovo, the idea of the leftist politics is very interesting, although political party political programs can hardly be understood, are not clear in these politics in the political daily in the country, the leftist parties in Kosovo are not close to the labor unions, even though they are called eyebrows are not active to stop social injustice, low discriminatory salaries, discrimination in employment of young people who come from the poorest classroom, only a party in the left in Kosovo called the

NISMA -Social Democratic Initiative has foreseen that from one family member without jobs should be employed a one member of the these family. In Kosovo there are still social assistance of 27 thousand families, and without health insurance of 90%, a small families have health insurance in alternative way in security companies. Through solidarity and support that homes have been built for homeless families. Most young people after completing high school enroll in public universities for free payment to enroll and attend the lessons. Around 25,000 young people enroll in faculties of public and private universities in Kosovo. In Kosovo, except the University of Pristina are founded other universities by the Democratic Party of Kosovo(PDK) with the coalition party as was the LDK and some others in coalition, five public universities was established , so Kosovo now has six public universities that were mainly established with political promises during pre-election campaigns since 2010, PDK even though it has the right program orientation it has acting as a left party, that this did not happen with the privatization even though there are still public interests in Kosovo such as Post Telecom, Kosovo Energy Corporation, which has been privatized some sectors. In Kosovo, most students enroll in public universities due to lower registration and attendance rates. While private non-public colleges have lower number of registered students due to high registration fees. Registration in private colleges is expensive for the Kosovo standard, an academic year in Kosovo in the private college's costs 850 euros, while PDK has freed the registration fee for new students for three years, even though this party calls itself orientated to program political right. Left program policies in Kosovo are growing, Self-Determination – "Vetvendosje" is a nationalist party that aims to unite with Albania declaratively, this political party is divided into two parts that have passed on the Social Democratic Party. In Kosovo are as well some minor political party with left orientations such are : The Movement for Union, in the 1990s, was the party of UNIKOMB, the People's Movement of Kosovo, the Kosovo Liberation Movement, while the Parliamentary Party had a right orientation and had operated in Kosovo until 2000 as a subject that was attached to a coalition with politically oriented to the center. Now in Kosovo do not function with LKCK as old name, now has changed the name in the Movement for Union that concerns the leftist programming policy that aims to unite Kosovo with Albania.

Development Policies in Kosovo

When there is no political development idea or vision then we have socio-political tensions and other emptying of negative energies.

7. Development policies or development vision

Development political idea or modality of policy thinking is a more important segment for countries that have been passed in a transition period, but as well some Western States have at times suffered from non-economic growth in the EU such as Ireland, Portugal, Spain and Greece, which they have big economic problems. But normal later, they have progressed quite well in terms of the economy, nowadays those are unemployed countries that behave in state-controlled limits. The stagnation in the development of the spheres of life comes as a result of the lack of adequate engagement and the potential of the political development vision. Kosovo's development policy is compared with some countries such as Macedonia, Albania, Moldavia etc., once in such a state of lack of ideas and perception, what is politics, and how to put the realities of the missing solutions. Once in this hopeless situation, Poland was faced with difficulties until become a member of EU. EU states helped to overcome the situation, then Romania, Bulgaria. As such crises arise as well as the Philippines, Ethiopia, etc. Lack of developmental ideas compatible with the socioeconomic circumstances of the state and the poor state budget, respectively, the economy behaves in other aspects to strike between economic criminality, political-social chaos and social development in general and the elements of enrichment without foundation and lack of order functioning and law. Parties cannot have a policy or vision if they are not tried to find them because "rhetorical words" without providing a solution "cannot be achieved solutions that everything starts from the idea eg. how to regulate or stimulate employment of citizens or how to regulate other areas. The impression is that there is "no one" in our minds or "no time" to offer realistic solutions or I can say the lack of courage as a result or concern coming from the aspect of non-knowledge. Sometimes when drafting development policies in Kosovo, there is missing information as well there is no- clear analysis, and non-clear statistics which are missing. Encouraging to reform or to make changes in development policies for certain sectors often happens because of the "fears" of "experimenting with it" and the budget is falling.

To do development policy, it is also required analytical courage and analytical expertise to access another approach. So there are some issues that do not depend solely on will but knowledge. Politicians who have no such ideas cannot bring about change. Changes do not occur in words but in the life sphere of the citizen. The institutions of Kosovo have not had clear ideas of development and vision but no courage during this period, no changes have been made except for political declarations but when they have seen and analyzed their relevance is missing political actions : they must try to come out with political proposal in some priorities sector but not to spend a lot of time in debate without solution, which in politics this should not happen because no government can change the whole life and whole social dimensions for a mandate but normal these changes are evolutionary.

A practical example , once had Ireland which has been faced with high unemployment and migration in EU countries to find employment but after a 10 year period on the basis of courage, but also knowledge and vision have come as a "wand" unemployed decrease to 4%. In Kosovo, for example, adequately unlikely to find the visionary model in this respect, for example: What to do with the extreme poverty and the budget allocated by the Government, except that all categories are slightly assisted and no one is protected sufficient as well as in the social aspect. The same situation is happening in health without the courage with the different approach to the public health sector, a great number of doctors in Kosovo work in the public- private sector , or a many medical workers or doctors they work in parallel in both sectors, or in politics employment as well as access to people to work with a relationship and to find it with a lawyer allowed by the state and to derive a law which in some way eliminates narrow throats and wild enrichment in all areas where it may find work , this is not tolerated. In poor countries, therefore, the situation is severe in the area of employment policies because low economic development trends do not provide opportunities. Or what to do with the teachers and their salaries, which always threating for protest and asking for increased wages as well have requested the public sector of secondary education. Can we as a state keep absolutely this way of organizing secondary education or to change the law for mix capital establishing school 50% public-private with the solid participation of citizens, apparently never thought of it. We need to analyze: Whether we can keep this whole public system in this formula normal that teachers in primary school and professors in secondary education remain dissatisfied and without a minimum stimulation then do not define what civil service is and what not? Even today, these questions have remained normal, as no one seems to think or gather "people with work" in this regard.

Parties eg. power comes without program and this program is expected by civil service designers, that's a mistake. The administration is a gatherer of information, analysis, but it is not said to make global development policy within the country as well reform with the same people as? Until yesterday they were the same! How can you work with the same people and wait for reforms? Politicians must be visionary of politics, but say we are politicians and experts, the impression is gained that these are the divided world. Developing policies are expensive for an international organization, local policy experts are paying 300 euros a day in Kosovo and in the west, do not talk as long as there are international policy experts who are paid 12,000 euros in Kosovo. How do I find political parties that are not a class of such expert business with designing electoral programs and platforms? When there is no paid-up by business structure to develop policy or to be near political parties . Hardly, it sounds like a lot. In Kosovo, the leader of the party has the votes, the others are treated as "workers", which support leader, who do not need to be paid at all mostly are volunteers and they are not happy to work for political parties without any interest , but they have to be "gratuitous" without payment, no political party enthusiasts, drawing volunteer programs or platforms for that reason they are not in politics because it "has to do it all". Political parties all over the world are made up of large capitalists, middle class, and poor class, or social classes or emerging labor parties different and expert or both of these components. So we are "pursuing" for development policy formulas.

It is enough that the parties in their programs define themselves and which economy class they represent, so what interests protect them? We have often spoken and drafted strategies but let's not forget many countries in Europe have failed with strategies but failed with projects development policies for particular sectors. And we must try the same thing. In Kosovo it's enough to be a professor at the University who teaches a book eg. 20 years and be called an expert, they are forgetting that they are teachers but without experience of practical development policies eg. it pushes policy experts with out-of-policy politics that no one works for a party that has no progressive vision for the sectors of life. Parties need to have clear ideas as they see their place in governance for their term. But there is hope if we know how to use human capacities. The party or program statutory reform should be in line with development guiding policies. For example, the LDK, PDK have the same programs with some small differences, AKR has an ad-hoc program just for the campaign for the central election that they have designed. AAK example . has started reforming the statutory-program, political action strategy as the only opposition with a parliamentary group with lack of development policies. Political parties often confuse the institutes they may have with councils. Advisory is for short-term recommending approach, the institutes are afraid. Institutes like the German Social Democrats and many others design politics and party views, this idea is now unproved in the parties of Europe and the US etc. The party's economic profile should be clarified to build development policies for particular sectors, otherwise, we remain ad-hoc in action, which party comes to power to work and rely on the state administration which is instructive and expects policy orders because policy provides development direction. there are legislative policies that do not allow money to be invested and invest in 'homes' and 'big' buildings where millions are in and there is no factory or money-making company, but all business is acting individually to build with those money there are many things that we have to think of in many other policies or take the agriculture sector there as in other sectors and politics, the land of bread is turned into garages, caravans, these are shortcomings that accompany us.

Time is moving forward, we do not dare to live in transition and wait for someone to know how to change the poor life of the citizen. We need to be determined, to unite the experts or to establish a government agency for development policies that will be stimulated good to continue the processes that have stalled in the country.

8. The state of serious reform in health

The severe social situation that reigns in these last ten years with the smallest possible reduction at least 15 % of extreme poverty, which poverty reaches the rate of over 16% and is not decrease at all, on the other hand over 52% of citizens are reportedly living below the level of living standards, it is an emergency situation that institutions should take concrete action to begin their sanctions. Predetermined grievances on all sides in some sectors such as: health, police, civil service and education workers are some dissatisfaction which are manifested and mentioned for years. The government as "always old", that the situation will be improved but it is still in critical condition with the possibility of exit from control. On the other side University in the private sector is threatened to sue the Government in courts even in international ones for the damage that will be made to their investments, normally that Your responsibility is the government regardless of justifications "Stopping the activity can be done only if it is in violation of law", and that no any basis in law. This situation is even more marked by the unemployment and the lack of prospects for the economic development of the state. While the Prime Minister has gathered around himself different offices, one of them even a little business development office seems to be sufficient support by the head of government or he is satisfied for sufficient support giving to him by Minister of Trade and Industry or the Minister of Ministry of Finance , the reasoning was that he is the prime minister who is engaged in the economic development of the country and we hope that this is the reason, because we are longing for the Government to function good and reasonable. The government time to time issuing an ad-hoc decision in contravention of the basic pension law to postpone retirement age for professors. Warnings from health workers and the state of affairs in the UCCK are an old story of our reality. The disappointment of the Kosovo Health Care Fund puts in serious condition over 70% of the citizens who are faced with life problems.

The lack of a fair access to the public sector of not finding a realistic and pragmatic plan for development policies in the field of health there's a situation here. In the field of health, it is required that as soon as the development program develops how the public health and the private sector will go. A model needs to be found that would encourage doctors and generally the public health sector to be more injected. The lines between the private and public private sector should be fully separated this could be the first option of a development policy plan, the second issue , public sector - benefit model is doctors to work only in the public sector, and the third model could be mix system, favoring doctors working in both the public and private sectors through the government program - drawing up memoranda for understanding between the Government and the private sector where they can use equipment from the UCCK by paying taxes. Workers working at UCC should have other income-generating opportunities; there are ways for this or comparative models. So to do more in this direction, otherwise, is the unbearable situation in this sector. The Ministry of Health needs to think clearly what to do in this direction to come up with a clear and urgent strategy to help the medical staff in this sector. The government has an obligation to start collecting funds as soon as possible for the health protection of the citizens where they will be assisted with institutional care through the health care. Money collection as soon as possible in this fund is and should be the uncompromising priority of state institutions. So however in the Assembly of Kosovo is not discussed with some special point about the serious state of public health of citizens in the last 10 years. It is surprising why civil servants did not stop for the fund because this could have been done by the pay they pay on tax.

Who lives well in Kosovo?

The economic development and the cost of the life of citizens, health and social services in Kosovo without any change is an assertion by the many organization in civil sector issued , after analysis and submission of these analytical papers which was made in several cities of Kosovo . This is the epilogue of the moment while the Government and the Assembly of Kosovo are dealing with laws and fruitless sessions, it seems to be easier for the government to draft laws while the executive government-Government deals with issues that have more to do with the control of public enterprises that are only profitable. While the private sector and the economy based in market it is completely in critical condition, the Chamber of Commerce is completely dissatisfied and BSPK because of the situation that has been created by bad policy, We can freely say there is a collapse of economic underdevelopment in the private sector.

An issue must understand that the public sector cannot consume the unemployed in Kosovo, because the state administration is not a continuous place to employ, while the private sector is completely no secure for salary of workers. We can reduce taxes by stimulating the economy and employment , regardless of the facts is necessary a soon passible to take measure to stimulate private sector. But who will take actions that could be indication directly to increase budget. once again for no development trend of private sector will not be welfare for citizens. If it reduces taxes only to enterprises in the private sector, taxation should be reduced for citizens as well, but the prices of the business community are not increased, especially for citizens to fall taxes or decrease for services such as electricity, utilities, , where does it take other than the citizens who are overcome by poverty, according to recent data this poverty is rising by more than 16% in extreme poverty while on the other side 53% of citizens live below the average level of life.

Who lives well in Kosovo.

At present, only 10-12% of Kosovo's business functions well, the public sector of enterprises accounts for about 8% of life with good standards such as PTK, the minimum wage ranges from 300 euros, to the airport about 350 euros, public sector salary in managerial positions reaches approximately 2500 euros for the leading staff of large public companies who are under the control of the Government, which has reached a full supervisory board and control and change management in this sector. The poor state is in education, health and social services. Professionals and teachers continue to live heavily by high school and elementary high school professors who have minimal salaries while unemployment over 43% is the biggest concern of ours. One thing to be surprised how the Government thinks when it will say that on the one hand teachers' salaries will increase and on the other hand proclaims that it will reduce taxes as a stimulus for the private economy sector, interesting though the Government is composed of theorists and other not well educated an who are mostly recognized as class which has survived from the private education sector, most of whom are professors at Private Colleges and Public Universities, but they are coming from business class. Economy have now come up to an interesting segment of the deformation of the market economy where bureaucracy and bureaucratic apparatus tends to take on the primacy of good living ... this it is a word when politics becomes the best business in Kosovo and when the state administration carries out the affairs of the politicians through their own government who plays that role as prime minister, who does not separate the duties from the prime minister and to delegate task, but one is knows that the role of a spokesman should be played by the important thing on this "Government" without a pronouncement, "but this is no longer important enough to control money, customs, and public enterprises by the key persons in government. In a survey conducted with citizens in seven cities of Kosovo on the question of who is living good in Kosovo the answer is : former professors and now current governors, PTK, Airport, some large companies in the private sector, "Dukagjini Company", Devolli Company,ETC Company, insurance companies. Kosovo's weak export never reaches ever from 6% to 7%, rising tax rates are increasing, and reportedly will be reduced to the business community. From which "tool" the government will come up to stimulate the economy and pay the teachers better and reduce the semester payments for students in the University of Pristina , which is well to reduce study costs? only up to 23,000 students can enroll in the universities, and that's all, and the private education sector is having big problems to survive, according to the majority number of students which are enrolled in public sector this time will remain on the road and remain without any commitment, normally that this can bring social deformities and serious consequences, we go further with a big rate of un-employment of students which finish the faculty. Another argument for the functioning of the government apparatus is of a centralized type and it works by making decisions and is not seen as grounded, while KEK has been given millions of euros of electricity but no electricity, although the temperatures are high at this moment reach up to 38 degrees behind the current is not enough. The level of health services is catastrophic without any change. We do not dare to work with ad-hoc and political decisions or political state-type policy directives has been a very interesting thing when the government tends to allocate salaries to municipal councilors apparently "the miracle never ends" where they still have to make a difference in a certain legal perspective, what is meant by the representatives of the Assembly of Kosovo and representatives of the Municipal Assembly, where it is known that both parties are representatives of the people when they add the given competences with the Ahtisaari plan the municipalities come out of "different stupid". Soon, it is expected that the 9 months report from the Kosovo Development Policy Institute will be released, then they will provide all the statistics obtained through the surveys, hoping that we will make a contribution for the Government to think better about how to manage and facilitate the lives of the citizens which is not quite enough good comment in public opinions . Some of the data published in this article are also taken from international organizations operating in Kosovo, they also claim misuse and corruption in this 9 month period, the latest Anti-Corruption Agency report also made this. Our idea as the IKPD is to help minimize the weaknesses of institutional functioning and not be seen only by the prism of the financial interests of the political functionaries. There are many "miracle " ascertained during this period also by various international organizations that I consider they will soon make public The press freedom and the public opinion is threatened reported threats from the guilty. But apart from this, there are some achievements such as road construction, although the intensity of construction has fallen in recent times, but there is progress, even here there is "qudira" inside the capital there are many unpaved joining roads as road construction has progressed of the villages. Another segment mentioned by citizens from surveys is that there are delays in establishing institutions or completing them. Such a report will soon be made public by the IKPD.

9. Unemployment is Kosovo's biggest challenge

If we analyze the process and the trend of unemployment in Kosovo has been totally disadvantaged in employment these nine years. The ability to find the right mechanisms in employment policies by the institutions has come to a degree or level of unemployment that is worrying. Unemployment is now reported to range from 39 to 43%, there is no exact figure that could create adequate employment strategies when it is known that a large number of unemployed do not even register at Employment Centers and do not attend trainings because of losing hope of finding a job. This is unluckily because of the interest in enrolling in job centers or attending vocational training. Not offering institutions an opportunity and stimulus has made the unemployed today not appear in these centers covering all municipalities. Inadequate employment policy and failure to put into effect a genuine and powerful legality that would help regulate the employment sphere has become itself. Lack of proper legislative infrastructure has allowed one to "have some work" and even switch jobs and businesses either public or private, while on the other hand the hard part does not have employment opportunities. This is today's reality in us. We need to engage in how to come up with an efficient employment or an adequate stimulation of enterprises to provide private sector co-operation and to encourage the interest of at least 15% of extreme poverty be minimized, at least approximately resolving the situation where the families in extreme poverty are required to be offered the real institutional opportunity for at least one member of the family to have employees and to eliminate nepotism and party politics in employment. There has been a lack of development policy incentives to undertake active operational measures to avoid the growth of extreme poverty, in addition, the strategy developed by the former Government has remained in the drawer of this Government, which at least should have been browsing to see the job that was once offered to alleviate extreme unemployment. While the Government is making efforts to establish control and oversight first on powerful public utilities such as PTK, which now has a "policy-making director" who will take care for certain employment of people, which should not do so, also the Airport Director was elected in the same way and the Director of KEK under strong government control lines, now in order even in A new director will be established in the Customs Administration, which means that it is too early to "let you sing it" to the Pension Trust Possibly even in that institution, the "Director" of the Trust, afterwards enabled the privatization fund of public enterprises with control, then the control over the institutions where "is the money" will be rounded up. So we have a powerful control and suffocation of the work of public enterprises where there is "no money" the most. This makes us understand a poor political and development philosophy, visible to the public and for the citizens of Kosovo to think in the queue for "money" control while on the other hand the citizens are left without social and health protection. Today, we are the only country in Europe where people are endangered by severe illness and illness and without any minimal social and health guarantee. The economic development so far has been overlooked, and no fiscal policy changes make us suspect the professionalism of is there anybody in Kosovo who is posing or opposed to what is happening in the social sphere where there are various manifestations of social diversity such as: growth of economic crimes, suicides, divorces, drug addiction, private-home prostitution and other forms which are present in social dimensions The Kosovo Assembly has not asked to be deployed on the agenda of what to become of the unemployed who reigns in Kosovo, why the Government is not called at least to report or to show why nothing is required to change in economic and social development in our country. There is surely the lack of will and the normal non-professionalism of MPs who are in their own best working on adding privates to themselves. One fact was that when MPs have a boost to increase their privileges while the government has been asked to deduct the costs, this is a phenomenon for the three mandates of the country's governments, while depicted a large number of them have received salaries of around 1400 euro per month, now when we add the possible official trips with "diplomatic passports", then the range of their privileges will be rounded. There is now a deputy that all the mandates have been MPs but "without resoult" for the citizens, if a survey with the citizens is made, it would be seen that most citizens will not even know the names of at least five deputies of the Kosovo Assembly. Who will solve the great puzzles and social deformities, unemployment in the state and bad affairs in the health field in Kosovo? Who among us will start to change these asocial trends and open the way to economic prosperity?

10. Political Parties and their Reform Ideas

Party reforms that are happening in Kosovo seem to be more compelling and trying to find opportunities for political reconfiguration in LDK and AAK, these reforms are being discussed but it is still not clear what can be reformed? And why? For example, in the LDK there are attempts to review the political cadres that can replace the deficiencies with the advances, in the AAK are expected substantial changes because they start from the Statute of the Party which means root change in the way of the organization and this is done in the way of getting of the ways to come up to the internal clarification of the political leadership and this change was proposed by the Statutory Changes Group, which had well analyzed the situation that has reigned and has become a determining factor for changing the political-normative-political norm of political leadership in AAK, there were rumors in this subject that this could well be different, I consider that Kosovo's political parties is "fought" to win the electorate, whether we want to accept or not the leaders in Kosovo bring votes but not the other leading members think the part the majority of the electorate have the leaders p the reform should take into account the extent to which Ramush Haradinaj is not satisfied with the work of the AAK parliamentary group "who is trying to push" AAK with advancing as the only real opposition in Kosovo and has witnessed a survey that AAK and Ramushin bring only 10% increase in Kosovo, this is fine but can be even better, the changes that Ramush demands that sometime have to bring somewhere according to its predictions and ideas AAK within this year will have a tendency to increase by 12%,

AAK's problem will remain giving access to professional political and business personalities and advancing business people in AAK policy without activating the business scale and presence in the leading AAK forums intellectuals, does not have much hope for major changes within the party however the efforts and dynamics that Ramushi has is changing matters it is essential that they do ,as well they another not have "other door to open ", "and" or they need to take up the intellectual class and the economic business class within the political forum or it will remain as AAK working with the same people today in the parliamentary group with many deficiencies, no more powerful professional personalities within the AAK parliamentary group, I think that the group for statutory changes is set for effective power and effective leadership and to emerge from some "political games", that have been in the past since have conveyed this political subordinate over a long period of time, this is what is called "political clarification in leadership", in Kosovo so will function and will function democracy for a period of up to two future institutional mandates. AAK is divided half of the member has fled from this party calling Ramushi's party of his brother and uncle. This party is rated as a family party. AAK's is only in Decan, AAK for now held this municipality, nowhere, in the next local and general elections AAK could be out of the political game in Kosovo and as well NISMA Socialdemokrate. There are some comments made in some media that AAK,PDK,NISMA has made the presidential system in the party this can happen freely in any other political parties, that does not mean to have an influence on Kosovo's central government because the word is only for parties at national level there is time to thought. Now coalition PAN is leading Government is a very unique bad governance which happen until now in Kosovo. In PDK there are no "even cosmetic" changes, but no idea to change something, their biggest concern is the positioning and satisfaction of internal political and institutional interests. The PDK leader is facing with "people of "with issues pertaining to positions in the Government, a part within this subject cannot" cope with servility ", a part or group within this party cannot see the advances of some of the most unpopular people in Kosovo or popular in odd ways, a part of PDK's presidency, disagree with past syndromes and "escalation in the back of the leader," there was the idea that "political aspirations" and getting "near of the boss" bring benefits to some personalities of this party cannot "very endure" this phenomenon. The PDK is concentrated in power leading the state , its entire political potential goes so far as to come to the conclusion: building and asphalting, building schools and closing private universities, there is little skepticism in the PDK as regards private universities, however those as universities there are enroll over 19,000 students who, if they are harmed, can almost can indicate to the electorate up to 100,000 sympathizers and in the midst of them a pious member of this subject, it means that "Hashim has a problem and Kadria ", although some aunt they are saying "good is the boss". The work of the ambassadors is one of the themes that could later shake even though it is said that President Thaçi now has a list of people from PDK for potential ambassador. Another important element is the PDK-LDK coalition, there are many "elbows" postponements, this does not make this coalition "lifestyle and survival" easy. From this analysis it is seen that the same political mind remains unchanged in Kosovo. The most exposed is concentrated in control and criticism, but not with ideas of what to do in development policy, this deficiency rests on both political opposition as opposition posit, or sometimes there are many essential mistakes that in the absence of knowledge in politics become mistakes and even produce counterproductive effects against development, this normally affects the economy and other areas. The most problematic subject are: unemployment, missing investment of foreign companies in Kosovo, poor economic development, health is in a "catastrophic", growing poverty, problem with energy, not good protection of social categories and without health security, bad local government developments. But for these areas time is needed to find ways and ways to get out of these heavy sites.

11. Left political orientation in education and health in Kosovo

Left-wing programs in Kosovo have no idea what should be the priority in the social treatment of social categories and even their programs do not have any major significance since only in the campaigns pre-emptive ideas and social views are heard as long as there is no choice losing their commitments to the social category. Citizens do not believe in their sincerity that they are seriously engaged in social issues and increase salaries of employees in the private sector. All these leftist parties do not have active social policy and there are situations where Kosovo citizens do not know clearly whether there are left or right parties in the commitments since the two left and right parties in pre-election campaigns promise wage growth, well-being social, health insurance, but after the pre-election campaign begins to say that there is no way to establish a health insurance fund, for five years in Kosovo it is about the establishment of this fund from the left and Kosovo still has no health insurance end today . In Kosovo for social policy from 2002 until today have set up the right-wing parties, these parties that have led the state have built a variety of social schemes, to date Kosovo has many established social schemes and over 280 million euros receive these schemes, 27 thousand families are part of the social assistance scheme, according to official statistics about 10% of poor and poor citizens for housing, clothes and food.

Kosovo has three older –homes: in Pristina, Skenderaj and Vushtrri, so far the state does not follow the practice of establishing old-age homes but according to analyzes and interviews with elderly persons Kosovo must have at least one old age- home for the municipality. Social services in Kosovo are decentralized, municipalities have the competence for social services but the budget is small municipalities, these schemes are still covered by the state budget.

The current qualification of political parties in the Kosovo-oriented left-wing programming spectrum:

11.1. Vetevendosje(VV)

There as three political parties in Kosovo who have been proclaimed left-handed parties for the time being "Self-Determination"(Albanian:"Vetevendosje"), is a party of unknown and inexperienced people in both level for general policies and social policies. In the leadership of these parties are also not recognized people from work with social and syndical categories, the relation of this party with unions or social groups is not known. This party even often calls different trade unions in Kosovo to support them as a left- party. This party is trying to have social democracy in formal declaration and with writing a letters without serious research. This party sometimes takes the lead on an ultra-nationalist party in country. The party's efforts are criticizing the other parties in government to win a much votes from citizens, but as a political party is completely inexperienced in government with the leading state, and to spent in good manner budget. It is estimated that it is difficult to win in election , but even if they win the governance and lead state,   the biggest problem remains the state institutions   needs to be reformed a lot. Or of the people that make up this party are the newly educated generations, and in democratic principles are with knowledge limits , its biggest victory of this party was in the local elections that won the lead with the Pristina municipality. This party after the 2017 parliamentary elections came out with a large number of deputies but it split into two parts. This party is facing huge staffing problems with un-professional people, more is a party that criticizes and organizes no social protests they are much focused against other political parties, even neither for May 1, they organize with the workers' syndicates protests or marches without participations of VV in this protests , usually as a party they deal with regional politics and with dialog Kosovo-Serbia for technical matters. VV are dealing with "high politics ", and have no capacity to lead dialogue with Serbia for normalization of relations. So this party is more problematic in country a much un-serious in ethical social issues. Its commitments do not reflect the social protection, policies of employees at work. They have some ideas that they gather on the internet and have opened debates during campaigns for establishing new funds for country, but the truth is that they have no knowledge for establishing fund nor that these funds to be useful for a tricky time for the citizens. But now, these social determinations are only faded during political campaigns for the elections at both levels but not for their daily activities on the political scene in Kosovo. This party has a largely uneducated and unavailable membership in the professional sense and what they are engaged in. LVV, describes PDK as a failed party in the government as predatory of public property and rarely have made improper scenes by playing with stones , either by running water rafts, gazelles in the Assembly of Kosovo, or have organized protests in front of the houses of former prime minister Isa Mustafa, have insulted that he shares with the speaker of the Assembly of Kosovo, Kadri Veseli and many officials of other parties, intellectuals, analysts , this critics against VV are describe with un intellectuals they peoples they have been rated   as extreme political movement and danger for Kosovo developments , but also problematic for Kosovo. A large number of activists of this party have been tried for attacks on Kosovo institutions. LDK and PDK treat them as an unresponsive individuals and unresponsive party and not responsive to the citizens of Kosovo for they political actions. "Vetvendosja" is declaratively engaged for national unification based on political documents that they have in papers, but this concept does not go forward at all, before that Albania is not interested at this moment and at all ready for a unifying political step in the Balkans with Albanians outside the state of Albania.

11.2. Political Program of "Levizja Vetvendosje"

Economic development

"Vetvendosje- Self-Determination" some part of engages : Development should   growth in production, employment for all citizens , which implies an increase in national income and creating   welfare for all citizens. The economic system should be in the service of citizens and not vice versa. VV are committed to another character of the state that is based on the social and economic development of the country and enables:

- economic growth

- sustainable development

- employment growth

- increasing the well-being of citizens

- increasing the capacity to increase the value of goods

VV will compile a long-term economic plan that serves as a guide to the entire economic activity within and around Kosovo. In this regard VV are committed to increasing the subsidization of the domestic economy to replace imports with domestic production and to increase exports. (comment: But is not saying how to do this or no explanations and other detail on this regard). Economic planning will be indicative: it will serve economic agents to orient their investments into enterprises that bring not only financial benefits, but also social benefits to all citizens. Production and Industry. Kosovo's wealth must be in the function of developing and enhancing the well-being of citizens rather than enriching politicians. VV commit, Kosovo- ourselves to have sovereign control over Kosovo's economic resources and development capacities. VV offer to build a mixed economic system in Kosovo, based on private and public enterprises. VV especially support those initiatives and private investment in the economy that demonstrate social accountability and guarantee for the country's development.

Kosovo needs the development of industry and production, to reduce the high unemployment rate, replace import and export growth, and increase its ability to create value-added products by developing capacity for production of final products the difference from the export of raw materials(comment without any clarifications how to do?). Mineral and underground resources of Kosovo should be used to promote industry development. VV are committed to a clear legal framework that guarantees the same conditions for all private entrepreneurs as well as a law against monopoly. For stimulation of local entrepreneurs and investments, Lëvizja Vetvendosje! supports the idea of creating entrepreneurial circles, where young entrepreneurs are offered simplified aid from all institutions jointly.

Privatization

Public politics of the economy and not private economy of politics

VV believe in the public policy. The public policy should not be expropriated because the public is perverted. Selling public property means harming the public interest. This is a consequence even if this was not the intention. "Western developed and democratic countries are also buying privatized enterprises"(comment: needs explanation) . In Kosovo are also sold profitable public enterprises! To the worse, privatization in Kosovo has been the opposite of liberalism: it has replaced the public monopoly with the private one[1].

 VV are opposed to the privatization of Kosovo's public enterprises and strategic assets that have great potential and are the basis of economic development of the country such as KEK (energy sources), Trepça with all mines (underground assets) PTK and against the concession award of Pristina International Airport.

VV are against privatization before:

- Decolonize, as social and public property in Kosovo has been violently transferred to Serbian public and social property through colonizing laws of the nineties;

- Take over and implement the current privatization fund since the hundreds of millions that have been collected from the sale of socially owned property in Kosovo are kept confined to the Central Bank of Kosovo and are saved to repay the owners of the property sold after to decide who they are;

- To have a long-term plan of economic, infrastructural and social development, since only then we will structure the economy;

- To have a strong and stable state because it will have the capacity to condition independent economic operators to comply with laws and regulations;

- To have the legal infrastructure set up because it eliminates the private monopoly and the dominance of the powerful in the economic sphere[2]. Privatization could eventually be part of the economic development guidelines and not the underlying principle and underlying principle, in which case the development would eventually be a consequence. VV are

---

[1] Levizja Vetvendosje ,short political program
[2] Levizja Vetvendosje ,short political program

committed to have a comprehensive assessment of the privatization process so far and the effects of this privatization. The sale of Kosovo's public and public property should be reviewed and revised if the procedures have been violated, and if objectively assessed that in certain cases the privatization has damaged the Kosovo economy; have violated human rights; be made as a result and / or through corrupt affairs (comment: Kosovo until now privatized almost 75% of enterprise, VV in the program request to revised all privatizations of eneterprise).

Vetevendosje (VV) and Agriculture

Planting land should bring us benefits rather than loss

VV commit ourselves to provide Kosovo farmers with the necessary economic space and the necessary financial and technical ability to work the land and to benefit from it[3]. VV will also take measures to increase farms, encouraging co-operation among farmers, in order to increase efficiency and yields from Kosovo's agricultural land. VV will make functional the professional agricultural institutes which will provide expertise for the best planting, cultivation and cultivation of agricultural land. We will also streamline the existing irrigation systems and invest in the construction of new systems to extend the irrigated land surfaces. Lëvizja Vetvendosje ! Categorically opposes the transformation of high quality agricultural land into construction sites. VV commit ourselves to ensure that the state guarantees agricultural products. Fiscal Policies[4].

Our taxes finance the state-building for everyone, not to benefit some of them.

VV commit ourselves to an escalated tax system, which differentiates between the value of use of different goods. There can be no VAT the same as for whiskey, as for milk. VV also commit ourselves to a progressive tax system, which differentiates between the different levels of income and wealth of the various members of society. Those who earn more would have to pay more for the overall welfare.

---

[3] Levizja Vetvendosje ,short political program
[4] Levizja Vetvendosje ,short political program

Kosovo's budget policies are at odds with the country's economic needs. VV are committed to increasing public investment in the country, but how there is not explaining at all in this program? As well as for more appropriately allocated budget funds but how?(comment: It doesn't has a explanations with details in this program). VV engage in investment in projects that benefit the economic development and welfare of citizens[5]. Kosovo needs to improve the legal infrastructure and enforceability of existing tax laws. In addition, we see the necessity to increase the tax base and combat informality in the economy. VV consider that the approximation of fiscal systems with Albania helps the economic development of both countries it is just declarative matter. VV are committed to integrating two fiscal systems into a tax and customs area it is declarative in base without any explanations.

Equality

11.3. Excluding a part of the company is the exception of a part of the opportunity

A country without large differences between groups and generations creates better living conditions and builds a more just and solidarity society[6]. Common wealth needs to be distributed even more equally. Those who have more and gain more should contribute more to the community than those with low incomes and with little or no wealth at all. Social equity strengthens the trust and solidarity on which a healthy society is built. VV are committed to more social equity and are committed to fighting poverty by increasing employment so that more people have the opportunity to live from their jobs[7].(**comment:** The program is not calculate how to do employment , if it is compare with unemployment around 35% of young people do not have job? How to fill state protection regarding on unemployment of this rate? So program

---

[5] Levizja Vetvendosje ,short political program
[6] Levizja Vetvendosje ,short political program
[7] Levizja Vetvendosje ,short political program

should explain more or less with details how to reduce level of unemployment?

As they says "Vetvendosje" aims for a Kosovo for all", not just for the rich people" it could be just formal declaration of this political party. Kosovo has approximately only 15 % which live with luxury other are middle class or poor. VV Therefore, they want the employees, both in the social and private sectors citizens , this is good and normally to have collective contracts, social security, health care, and trade union rights guaranteed by law[8]. But how ,private sector is not function without economic trouble ,they functions with loans, they do not have enough money even to pay sometimes workers? And some rich people in this sector even they do not pay salary during summer vocations such is private college in Kosovo which they do not pay professors during three month until November. Easy is to say but how to solve this matters? Vetvendosje engages the threatened layers to rely on public social assistance systems funded by a progressive tax system). VV commit ourselves to create the necessary space for equal engagement of women in the social, political and economic life of the country. VV also commit ourselves to regulating the state by law, and to fund mechanisms that encourage gender equality and the various social strata.

Social Policies and Pensions

11.3. The state should take care of each citizen

VV consider the pension and social assistance as right, not as a favor of power[9]. The state must take care of all social categories that are impossible to survive without the help of the state.

Comment: The problem is concrete how does this political party resolve the solution for the poor, how much are Kosovo's budget capacity to solve problems, how to feel well the Kosovar pensioner a basic pension of 75 euro of a pension , citizens   get out of work pension 250 euros

---

[8] Levizja Vetvendosje ,short political program
[9] Levizja Vetvendosje ,short political program

most, when it is known that a Kosovar pensioner if he does not have additional income from the family he can have a big trouble , does not eat enough food and clothes, from the 250 euro pension he get one pensioners' which he works almost half of his life , Kosovar citizen nearly 100 euros pays different taxes, water tax, electricity tax, taxes for berths, taxes for public television, but even worse for pensioners in the scheme of 75 euros who are in a state of emergency in Kosovo. The main problem for VV is that this party in its program does not give concrete explanations of how the solution is solved, not just the demagogic vocabulary, usually such programs have all the other parties in Kosovo who declare and promise to resolve, but when should they start solving social problems for what they engage then failing even to make a program. But what about the state for the retirees, the social scheme and citizens' contributions are lacking, so with this pension trust and with this pension fund even does not govern the state, the money of the citizens of Kosovo are used for international investments around the world and that money of this the fund has no data nor where it is found, the truth about this fund is that the money of the Kosovars is exploited for investments in international enterprises but the growth of the pension capital is minimal, there is no transparency for the work of this trust. Both party and VV party have requested that this money be invested in Kosovo and not outside but until now there is no movement in this direction.

 In this regard, VV commit ourselves to provide Kosovo pensioners with a monthly pension that meets their needs and enables them a dignified life[10].

Comment: It is just a declarative and wish, how to do this with this economic development in Kosovo? The policy is to solve problems not just to mention them. Kosovo's policy programs are more demagogic than an obligation for a political party in the country to solve matter concerning to the citizens.

---

[10] Levizja Vetvendosje ,short political program

KLA war veterans, KLA invalids, family members of the fallen martyrs, political prisoners and persons with disabilities will have special legal treatment as well as other facilities in their confrontation with every day.

VV and Education

Every citizen has the right to have equal opportunities for quality education.

The right to education is universal, inalienable human right, and society must provide everyone with the opportunity of education. Public education at all levels should be free for everyone. Vetvendosje(VV) is committed to increasing the quality of the public education system and to rigorous quality control of teaching in all sectors and all levels of education. Public education should be seen as fundamental, while private education as complementary[11]. Vetvendosje requires an education system that promotes school achievement regardless of ethnicity, social and / or gender[12]. Kosovo Laws should adopt the UN Convention on the Rights of the Child, which obliges the social authorities of member states to investigate the needs of children in the compilation and implementation of all relevant laws[13]. Our schools must contribute to the creation of a healthy society, guided by the universal principles of justice and social solidarity. VV want to have schools for adults in which the lesson is organized that enables him to follow him without getting rid of work or other daily engagement.

Vetvendosje considers that the state has an irreplaceable role and opportunity in the development of science and technology[14]. In this regard we are committed to the creation and funding of scientific institutes in all those scientific areas for which Kosovo needs and capacities[15]. VV commit ourselves to create conditions for all our compatriots to make the academic and professional preparation abroad

---

[11] Levizja Vetvendosje ,short political program
[12] Levizja Vetvendosje ,short political program
[13] Levizja Vetvendosje ,short political program
[14] Levizja Vetvendosje ,short political program
[15] Levizja Vetvendosje ,short political program

available to serve the state and society in Kosovo. VV will engage in additional education for migrant children.

VV and Health program

The state must guarantee and finance the health of citizens

VV engages employees in the public and private sector to be offered social and health insurance in collective contracts. This insurance should be public and managed by public companies[16]. At the same time, it is necessary to invest in the public health sector so that health is the right of everyone and not just the privilege of some. We strongly believe that the cost of the health system will gradually decrease with increasing health care and through additional investments in the preventive culture of the disease. This is achieved through various social institutions: family, school, media, etc. Above all, and above all, we need a healthcare system that has the material benefits and professional preparation for a comprehensive and effective preventive system[17].

11.4.Social Democratic Party

PSD was founded in the 90s, this party was close to the LDK, although its orientation is left while the PSD party with the leftmost program .VV divided into two parts, 12 MPs separated from the Vetëvendosje Movement and they have talked to PSD and now are they become a part of this party. Until now PSD do not any significant role in Kosovar policy , now this party is coming empowering because of 12 deputies Parliaments of Kosovo are now member of this party. A party has elect a new president of PSD from people which was transferred to PSD .VV is divided in two main part .PSD now is expected to see whether there will be any political massiveness though there even is great skepticism that it will get more win percentage on the political scene in next election in both level. Kosovo now has interesting parties in the Social Democratic area .

---

[16] Levizja Vetvendosje ,short political program
[17] Levizja Vetvendosje ,short political program

Movement for Union

The Movement for Union is a party of orientation of the program's left in Kosovo politics once called the name LKCK Kosovo's Kosovo Liberation Movement transformed into a party that wants unification with Albania, this party is in coalition with PDK in the previous Government , is now an opposition party. There is a small political structure and there are some people who were part of the KLA, for the time being out of the political game in Kosovo. This party thinks it would be solution for Kosovo a national unification solution.

12. The Perspective of Left Political Orientation

The political outlook of the political left is not clear, for the moment the political party in Kosovo does not have the orientation of the class representation, mainly all the parties often become unclear with political programs. It is take time and years to have programs to clear parties in Kosovo. The left party in Kosovo has difficulty to build a social state for the citizens in the absence of an extremely weak market economy. It is almost difficult to build different social funds and build capacities social situation with this weak economic development. Although there may be a different future altogether. The left political parties in Kosovo is good for existing so as well there is no harsh criticism of the logic of the right parties because at this stage it is very early to happen division on a political basis. In Kosovo there is no economic class built until now, and there is no adequate class representation in state institutions. For the moment all the parties are fighting the same for power and governance with. The state that is composed of the current party as left-wing is a poor-class economist or a professor.

The Democratic Party of Kosovo

The Democratic Party of Kosovo is a popular right party founded on traditional, and national , on the values of the liberation war in Kosovo and the universal values of civic democracy.

 The Democratic Party of Kosovo was established in the Founding Assembly held on the date12/10/1999.The party's official name is the Democratic Party of Kosovo. The PDK aims to develop Kosovo as a free and democratic country, based on the rule of law (comment: This party is very criticize in Kosovo, many officials of this party are involved in corruption).

PDK : In constitutional and parliamentary democracy, in a strong and functional state, with a free economy of market, which guarantees the fundamental rights and freedoms of citizens, respects the constitutional values, traditional, moral, historical and national, protects human dignity, family, and private property entrepreneurship[18]. The CCP is strongly committed to affirming and guaranteeing the freedom of thought, expression, solidarity, social equality and personal responsibility of every citizen, the principle of equal opportunities and protection of civic values and ethnic and religious diversity of society[19]. DCP is a continuation of the values of the liberation war and continuously engages in the promotion of by strengthening the state of Kosovo and aiming at national integration and the protection of rights legitimate Albanians living outside the state borders of the Republic of Kosovo[20].PDK aims to compete through free and democratic elections, respecting the values democratic and free voting principle, leading and strengthening the rule of law, and more integration swift republic of Kosovo in the Euro-Atlantic structures and its dignified representation everywhere on world.

The PDK's vision is to make Kosovo a proud and European country. In this regard PDK aims at:

- To have an independent, democratic and sovereign state;
- To saw a modern democratic republic based on the principle of the separation of powers, the rule of law, the building of a modern democracy, the rule of constitutional values, respect for the freedoms and the rule of law human rights and minority rights guaranteed by the Constitution, with laws and conventions international. To develop a free market economy, through the principle of market liberalization and competition free in it;

---

[18] The Democratic Party of Kosovo, Statute, Article 3
[19] The Democratic Party of Kosovo, Statute, Article 3
[20] The Democratic Party of Kosovo, Statute, Article 3

- To build relationships with the United States of America, integrate
- The Republic of Kosovo in the European Union, NATO, the UN and other mechanisms international;
- Establish a sustainable, professional and efficient national security system by cooperating with the European Union, NATO, the United States of America, the neighboring countries and those of the region, to enable a sustainable security environment for all citizens of the Republic of Kosovo;
- To protect the interests of the state and citizens of the Republic of Kosovo, respecting the order constitutional, legal and international agreements[21].

Internal Democracy in PDK

The PDK functions on the basis of the principle of internal democracy, which is expressed through the right to be elected and to be elected in all PDK bodies and on the basis of the vote principle equal to all members and respect for the right to express and promote the opposite opinion. Each new PDK member has the right to express his views and opinions, but the decisions taken most of them are mandatory for all PDK members[22].

Other activities :

PDK, in addition to party activities, in accordance with the Constitution and the applicable laws, organizes social, political and economic activities, clubs, forums, institutes and study organizations with purpose of its benefits. All PDK activities are public , except when determined unlike the Statute or any other act, this applies both inside and outside the territory of the Republic of Kosovo.

---

[21] The Democratic Party of Kosovo, Statute, Article 4
[22] The Democratic Party of Kosovo, Statute, Article 10

Bodies and mandate

1.PDK is organized in central and local bodies[23].

2. The central organs of PDK are:

a. The General Convention,

d. President ,

b. The Steering Council (KD),

c. Presidency ,

the National Assembly (CA).

3. The mandate of all PDK bodies is four (4) years.

4. The organization of Democratic Women (GD), the Youth Organization

Democratic (RD) and Volunteer Groups (GV) of PDK.

Political Program of PDK

Market Economy

- PDK is committed to private economy in Kosovo based on market economy laws open and free, integrated in regional and Euro-Atlantic institutions. This perspective e it will generally determine its political, legislative and administrative orientation.
- PDK will engage in the privatization of social property as soon as possible after free elections.
- PDK during the transitional phase will make the utmost efforts to say the consequences of war and reduce the economic backwardness that characterizes our country in relation to Europe. To achieve of these objectives PDK is committed to the spirit of the Stability Pact for South Eastern Europe donors and foreign investors to facilitate the implementation of their projects do with Kosovo.

---

[23] The Democratic Party of Kosovo, Statute, Article 20

- PDK is committed to adapting our economy to new circumstances, whether with the European context like the world. Creating a flexible market is one of our objectives.
- Whereas free competition in the market and freedom of exchange are indispensable to stimulating increasing economic growth, PDK is committed to a strong and competitive market.
- For this reason, the existence of a framework that will enable market forces to comply with Correct their role, is indispensable for economic success, and is a condition for an efficient employment policy.
- In the world where globalization and scientific progress have not stopped, the party must create conditions which will enable enterprises to prosper and adapt, which will favor also the creation of new companies.
- PDK will stimulate, favor and facilitate the creation of enterprises by facilitating and facilitating mitigating administrative measures ....
- The development of small and medium enterprises is an absolute priority because, in these enterprise is the biggest potential for productivity growth and job creation.
- PDK will orient society towards the modern economy and engage against each the overthrow of innovations.
- Whereas free competition in the market and freedom of exchange are indispensable to stimulating economic growth, PDK is committed to a strong and competitive market[24].
- As the new technologies radically modify the nature of the work and give the organization working an international dimension, PDK considers that one of the most important tasks is means modernization, should be, investment in human capital, so that individuals and social and economic enterprises from the new technological innovations in Kosovo and the region, will be perceived with a dozen of uncertainty about the employment of people. For this reason PDK will is committed to the creation of

---

[24] Political program of PDK

conditions of continuous professional training, according to market needs.

Social dimension

- PDK aims to protect the poor and mediocre social strata on which they tend the consequences of the war. Particularly the families of martyrs, political prisoners and victims of Serbian aggression.
- PDK will be especially committed to helping them and to integrate them densely friends .
- PDK is committed to institutionalizing a new social spirit that consists in creating conditions equal to the progress of every citizen of Kosovo.
- The unemployment period should be extended over a period of time to improve the qualification professional.
- PDK will strive to respect the minimum social norms, help families to adapt to comply with the changes and to offer new opportunities to those families that cannot follow evolution.
- To create a wholesome welfare of the people we will engage;
- to open a new perspective for the citizens of Kosovo,
- to open new jobs,
- to enable new qualifications that will be in line with European standards,
- The PDK will be committed to providing all retirees with the right to retirement, this universal social and human right.
- PDK will have continuous care for political, all-time, persecuted families of wizards, war invalids and all those who in various forms have suffered from the conqueror. PDK will take care of the employment of members of the Kosovo Liberation Army.
- PDK is committed to finding the most appropriate ways to combat the problems ever with urgent with regard to criminality, social integration, the use of narcotics and all other deviations in society[25].

---

[25] Political Program of PDK

Comment: PDK as other political parties in Kosovo is interested to have development of market economy, even this party is to much criticized from intellectual people in Kosovo about controlling of public enterprise in Kosovo and Court system.

PDK program : Female and children care

- In full compliance with the Universal Declaration of Human Rights, resolutions, UN Declarations, Conventions and Recommendations as well as specialized institutions that have for the purpose of eliminating all forms of discrimination PDK will engage the children to Regardless of ethnicity, religion, gender or race, to ensure a happy life and with perspective.
- PDK will advocate for the right of children to be protected by law, to provide children with protection social for normal psycho-physical development, children enjoy the right to compulsory primary education free.
- PDK will engage children in both the city and in the village to create conditions for learning, defensive and various cultural and recreational activities.
- PDK will be committed to stop the work and exploitation of children of the age by law who are under.

Youth

Youth was the main pillar of our liberation war, it will be the cohesive force of society in Independent and Democratic Kosovo.

- PDK sees the necessity of comprehensive youth support, education, employment education and its involvement with priority throughout the country's political and social life. Special care will dedicate their professional upgrading, employment and specialization to the world external.
- PDK will stimulate young people for recreational and sports activities.

EMANCIPMENT AND WOMEN'S RIGHTS

- PDK is committed to the emancipation of society in general and of women in particular.
- PDK highlights the role and importance of Albanian women during the liberation war.
- The PDK will commit itself to having the same gender-equivalent work for a work of equal value and will fight against any form of discrimination of women in this regard as well as in all other aspects.
- We will commit ourselves to taking all necessary measures including the provisions legal action to combat all forms of trade with women and prostitution as deformities modern society.

PDK program : Health Policy

PDK is committed to maintaining and improving the health of all citizens as a duty to the creation of a healthy society in Kosovo. In order to do this, the health policy will be based on health planning such as the main task towards full restructuring of the health system through global and coordinated policy without forgetting the priority in allocating the means in the framework of this policy.

Democratic League of Kosovo **(LDK)**

LDK is a party with a right-wing program; the founders of this party were political figures of former communists transformed into the founding of a party based on a market economy and capitalism similar to Western states. This party for more 17 years had a generation old politics that their expedition originated from the former communist system that had been established among Kosovo Albanians as a popular all-cause news papyrus for liberation from Serbia. Since 1996, it had a greater impact on the civic opinion of Kosovo, whereas after 1999 this party was more locate in political party than before as political movement such was before during the events of 1990- 1999 in Kosovo.

11.5. LDK for economic development

LDK believes that private initiative, competition and open market are the main forces that provide economic prosperity. In this regard, the role of Parliament and the Government is to provide a legal framework within which these activities are conducted. Right for free entrepreneurship and to realize profit also involves the obligation either solidarity with all those involved directly or indirectly in that activity Entrepreneur. Through the interaction of entrepreneurs with the state, financial institutions, education and training and social policies, enables internal cohesion economy and society. Based on this philosophy, LDK is strongly committed to strengthening its economy market in Kosovo, to promote competitiveness and integration into regional markets and global. The spirit of entrepreneurship, which is part of the philosophy and survival of the people of Kosovo over the years, should be promoted in all policies. New population e Kosovo is the most valuable asset Kosovo has. On this basis, development policies should be in the function of continuously increasing the quality of education. In compliant with European standards, the environment for the generation of entrepreneurial ideas, attracting foreign investment and promoting employment. However, economic development is sustainable, if resources used rationally and everyone benefits from development. LDK's economic policies will create conditions for improving the quality of life of all citizens. The eradication of poverty will take center stage in politics LDK governance. All Kosovo citizens should benefit from the system comprehensive health and social policies. Provide public services quality and the building of transparent institutions remain a matter of principle in governance. The main challenge for future governance remains the transformation of Kosovo's economy from an import-based economy into a domestic-based economy, export promotion and knowledge. In this regard, the challenge remains the strengthening of competitiveness, increased productivity of local entrepreneurs and active involvement in international markets. Eliminating barriers to business and private entrepreneurship is the key to this transformation of Kosovo's economy. LDK's economic policies aim at creating equal conditions for investment, through road infrastructure, telecommunications, energy and water, in order to create conditions for a harmonious development and overcome the regional differences in Labor market. LDK considers that economic development belongs to all citizens of Kosovo, inside and outside it, will therefore ensure an active involvement in the development economic development of our fellow countrymen, working and living in other countries.

Private sector development

A dynamic private sector enables young people to create their own countries work. Advancing the knowledge economy and strengthening local competitiveness is an important prerequisite. Stimulating domestic production and quality improvement local products and services is the first step toward reducing addiction from imports. The global market and competition is gained initially by competing in the market local imported products. Foreign investment plays a key role in increasing the productive potential of the economy Kosovo. LDK believes that increasing production capacities, job creation, improving trade balance, and improving product quality and I services are achieved faster through policies that make Kosovo a country of destination foreign investors. LDK is committed to empowering the legal framework it protects foreign investors, just like local investors. A safe and sustainable financial environment enables the realization of ideas entrepreneurs through the provision of favorable credit conditions. LDK commits to increased competition in the financial sector and increased efficiency of the operation justice system and investor protection, convinced that these measures will enable the lending conditions of entrepreneurs to be more affordable. Mobilization of privatization funds and the Pension Fund creates development potentials, but should be preceded by a national strategy for exploiting and guaranteeing them funds.

Improve the legal framework and reduce bureaucracy in relation to businesses

LDK is committed to eliminating legal barriers that hinder the development of by promoting the freedom of movement of people, goods, and capital and services. The legal framework should be assessed on a regular basis for its effects and change according to developments in the market. LDK will insist on a role added to the local authorities in providing the facilities of doing business, enabling decentralized legal framework and the necessary discretion of local authorities, for to foster their competition for attracting businesses to their localities.

supporting small and medium enterprises About 99 percent of enterprises in Kosovo are small and medium-sized enterprises (SMEs), which employ over 80 percent of private sector employees. The ability of these enterprises to operate and adapt to market conditions ensures it income for the large number of employees in these enterprises. LDK is committed to the establishment and operation of SMEs should be much easier on a bureaucratic basis.

Investing in human capital and promoting innovation

The large number of young people in Kosovo is a prerequisite for a power economy dynamic workers. But, this resource can only be enabled by offering it quality education, flexible to market requirements and diversifiable. In this direction, LDK is committed to a market of educational institutions with the opportunity to public and private education, which reflects the market needs of competing skills and for the application of European standards. Such an educational system enables creation of innovative and capable people to adapt to change fast and continuous market needs. Must invest in incubators business and should especially rely on ideas and business cooperation in the midst of Diaspora and Kosovar businesses.

Agriculture, rural development and tourism

Agriculture remains a very important sector for promoting employment in Kosovo, to increase the income of many families in rural areas and reduce poverty. Moreover, the high dependence on consumption of foodstuffs by imports and imports. Kosovo's deep trading deficit can only be improved through growth domestic production in agriculture. LDK is strongly committed to promoting the chain producer, from primary agricultural production, to processing, storage and marketing agricultural products, as well as stimulating and subsidizing credit and improvement measures of public infrastructure. Coverage of the local market with agricultural products from the country, is the first step of supporting local production. The LDK considers it very important to exploit the rich tourist, with in order to promote the sustainable and harmonious development of tourism through affirmation and preserving values such as: country tradition, culture, folklore, archaeological treasury, cities museums and historical monuments. Priority will be given to programs and facilities tourism, which provide tourism opportunities linked to neighboring countries.

Taxes policies

LDK will be committed to developing fiscal policies in line with the criteria of which derive economic objectives, stimulating new investments, employment and the withdrawal of external capital. LDK estimates that high taxes discourage productive investment and harm employment. Taxes should be as much as needed to cover the core functions of state, leaving citizens and businesses to decide for themselves how to invest their income. The application of a simple tax system remains a priority of LDK, while respecting the principles of fairness and equal treatment of taxpayers by distributing the tax burden proportionally. LDK believes there are enough space in Kosovo for increasing budget revenues through combating informality and fiscal evasion.

Public Expenditure

LDK is committed to a small and efficient government and public sector, with departments governmental organizations that are functional and of the optimum size, in accordance with the needs for services to citizens and businesses. The LDK believes in the budget policies they keep the sustainability of the state budget. LDK is committed to a financial discipline with regard to the state budget for it ensuring that future generations do not bear the burden of spending that is happening right now. This approach ensures fairness in the allocation of fiscal burden.

LDK Program: Public enterprises

LDK is committed to responsible and professional corporate governance that ensures the sustainability of public enterprises, high quality of services to citizens and economies of scale providing services at lower cost than the sector private. Continuous control and monitoring, audits and periodic application I the performance assessment mechanisms of public enterprises will promoted.

LDK Program :Education and Science

LDK's vision is for Kosovo to develop towards an integrated, knowledge-based society in the European course of education and science. Such a society is built through equal opportunities for education and personal development for all citizens. LDK is committed to an inclusive education system that provides conditions for qualitative training and in accordance with the needs of the labor market and society. LDK considers education as one of the main determinants of progress and long-term economic and social sustainability of the country. LDK is committed to integrating Kosovo education into the European Space of Kosovo Education.

LDK will provide opportunities for young people to make the choice for general education or professional, in line with their objectives and their interest and the labor market. Promoting Entrepreneurship Skills in Educational Curricula at all levels and educational profiles, the LDK considers it fundamental to generate ideas young people and hiring young people who finish school. That's why it will lifelong learning is promoted to enable renewal of knowledge, in line with the development trends of the economy sectors. The LDK will support the development of the private sector in education at all levels and will develop policies of strong competition between the public and private sectors, while respecting the European and world values of education. LDK estimates that science and research should be promoted and supported projects and publications of scientific institutes and to support scientific research independent scientific and higher education institutions. LDK e considers it of particular importance to create an integrated system for exploitation efficient research and scientific creativity of Kosovo and Kosovo's integration into Kosovo.

European Research Area

LDK will engage in the quality and effectiveness of education at all levels and be integrated, including the training and transition system from school in quality work with the aim of creating a motivating working force with high versatility. Facing the challenges of globalization and the vision for knowledge society will be ensured computerization and digitization of schools and standards for evaluation will be created and internal quality monitoring of education. LDK is committed to the permanent increase in the education budget, taking into account the new population of Kosovo and the greatest need for education. Participation of Expenditure on Education in Gross Domestic Product (GDP) and on Expenditures general government should behave above the European average, due to demographic specifications of Kosovo. DK is committed to the right resolution and advancement of the employee's status education at all levels and make radical improvement of working conditions.

LDK program -Health

As a builder of an authentic health system that kept alive for years, long occupation, care for the health of the population of Kosovo, LDK has priority high development and advancement of the health system. Based on European standards, LDK promotes an efficient and resource-based healthcare system sustainable, ensuring equal access to healthcare services for all citizens. Reducing the degree of morbidity and mortality by increasing the quality of health services, according to contemporary standards, is a primary goal. Kosovo has a great need for capacity building for primary health care, for family health education and for the implementation of the information system health. LDK is committed to an integrated health management at all levels, with clear and efficient referral systems. LDK estimates Kosovo needs a master plan to ensure adequate distribution of medical infrastructure medical staff throughout the country. Building an IT system, functional healthcare system that integrates all stakeholders is the first step towards this master plan. Sustainable health financing will be ensured through expanding resources financial, through the addition of public funds for health, application of the scheme health insurance, as well as promoting public-sector partnerships and private ones. The LDK believes that the funding scheme should reflect the growth of quality which will be affordable for citizens. LDK is committed to the overall integration of the health system throughout as well as the achievement of inter-municipal standards regarding the number of personnel medically relative to the population. In addition, LDK is committed to advancing family medicine to target diseases that can be eliminated in the most way effective in the early stages through better family health outcomes.

Social Policies and Interconnect Solidarity

As the center - right party, the LDK promotes the strengthening of the market economy and economic development as the main tool for alleviating poverty and unemployment However, in a country where poverty is extreme with close to half of the population poverty, it is necessary to ensure inter-societal solidarity through policies economic redistributive income. LDK believes that dynamic development and adaptation to global markets should be compatible with the principle of social responsibility which has the society towards certain groups, as this is the way to achieve cohesion necessary social and economic development that ensures sustainable and long-lasting development. To ensure a sustainable social protection, the social protection scheme and pension scheme should be organized in three pillars. The first pillar has to do with building. Social Insurance Fund, based on taxpayer contributions. The funds of this fund should be used to promote the employment of the unemployed. The second pillar has to do with pension insurance, where, in addition to compulsory pension insurance, voluntary savings schemes are also promoted. The third pillar includes assistance social welfare that provides the state for the poorest, which should ensure that the family, with the means that they receive, meet the elementary needs. As much as possible, social assistance will be conditioned by the active work of the beneficiaries in different public works and private, and with participation in various trainings. This is the best way to mitigate poverty and reduce dependence on social assistance in the long run. LDK is committed to building a sustainable socially-owned scheme in the long run tall. High unemployment has made the number of contributors relatively low small, compared with the number of beneficiaries of social insurance. Must be eliminated in maximum obstacles that discourage companies from taking women at work and having to encouraging the employment of elderly people who have not yet reached their retirement age. LDK engages in active social policies and promotes entrepreneurship for it reduce dependence, from social schemes. Therefore, as a tool for mitigating unemployment and poverty and consequently dependence on social security, initiatives will be promoted young and female entrepreneurs. This will be done through the creation of incubators business, financing schemes for businesses established by groups marginalized, providing counseling and training for young and female entrepreneurs etc. In rural areas in particular, alleviating poverty and reducing dependence on assistance social development will be done through the provision of opportunities for intensive development in agriculture and other incentives in the field of agricultural lending. LDK considers it to be cautious special deserves workers affected by the privatization of socially owned enterprises, in so that they do not become a burden of social assistance. LDK is a member of the European People's Party.

11.6.LDK and PDK coalition of right orientations of political parties

The LDK with the actions so far in this Government is more left than right, this is seen with the added concern of this Government in the social sphere. Thus, social issues, social schemes and health aspects are very positive, we have a positive social advancement in Kosovo, we can say that it goes to quality and well-being, syndicalist always was satisfied during of LDK. When considering social and health policies, both government departments, such as the Ministry of Labor and Social Welfare and the Ministry of Health, are ministers led by the LDK they take care much about social aspect. The MEF's has central role so far have played these two ministries and the Ministry of Finance, that was deals with all things that can be fulfilled in social aspect .MF minister has decide for all the economic development in Kosovo. Big mistake, this ministry allocates budget to the ministry, receiving fiscal policies and other things that this Ministry has undertaken most of them belong to the Ministry of Economic Development, but we have seen a strange role of this Ministry, which its powers are allocating budgets for ministry officials and taking care of a genuine state financial government. The powers of this Ministry to allocate a budget in accordance with the Government's program, in the regulation of the work of this Government, in Section 7.1.1 states:

"The Ministry of Finance is dealing with the purpose of thoroughly examining the direct or indirect effects of the proposal on public spending or in the economy." But there are other wonders when this minister deals with most of the things he is not called and tries to stand on the policies of other ministries. This leftist Kosovo government, made up of rightists, is impressed that there is no economic development, but it is more common to deal with social and health problems, I would like to emphasize an important factor, but also very strange when it is said have employed 18,000 new workers, great surprise for sure this government can boast of a large number of government departments in total 21 ministers, China has a prime minister and 4 deputy prime ministers and a secretary general and has 23 ministers in the portal its official and we are well with number of ministers, almost like China with number.

Very little with economic development and it seems that we have enormous employment in line with economic development. Suffice to go to the capital to see how local leases are rented, full of business premises are empty, there is nothing from private sector development, so what has been done so far, just words and nothing more. It is not good to say so much employment that I have the impression, as well as most of the citizens, that the proclaimed employment is far away, this is evidenced by the Statistics Agency. So what is this job? Do you want to say without being a? So there is enormous employment without a match with the market economy, if this government is thinking about party employment in boards and civil service and diplomatic service, who have hired as much as possible, here we agree that it is true, as they could, even when it ' they could have left it for later. So the Right Government, the Government of Business, how much private enterprise this Government has driven in economic development. Did this government release the newly-established businesses for at least 2 years from taxation, or it has been fired at the NGO sector that this sector does not even exist. Of the 9,000 NGOs, nearly 20 are not functioning, so 95% of them are function and do not work at all. This Government NGOs treat them legally as businesses like, so civil initiatives have come to an end, they are almost all extinct. Almost 900 NGOs has been registered this year, maybe next year, unless they run without revenue, otherwise they cannot pay for office rent, what about this topic? The proclaimed economic development is completely failed, just what can the business itself develop, the unmanageable fiscal escalation, it does not know, any reform such as law should be applicable if it is not accepted by the market, private enterprises Most trading does not implement fiscal reform, otherwise the private sector goes bankrupt. We have the hope at least the social side can be improved and if the law on effective health insurance enters in force , we are in great profit as a citizen, otherwise all the way down!

Does this government understand itself as being left or is it saying it is right? I would say, when rightists become left, right in a poor state, over 50% poor in Kosovo , extreme poor 12%, only 18% of citizens live dignified and normal lives and in luxury. These classes are: the political one and a number of businessmen associated with power, so Kosovo is a state where most citizens go to the sea and feed on bank star cards and every second on loans with abnormally high return rates. It is easy to talk and talk, but to act in the framework of economic development we are far away. If we add that the Assembly has been blocked for a long time now, and now it has five or six last sessions held as in communist times without criticism, without anything, then what is this orientations ? In the meantime, LDK and PDK sent a contingent of party ambassadors, full of party boards, full of public universities without a framework, some 270 doctoral candidates are expected to be enrolled at a private university in Albania, over 80% are party parties and among them there are judges and whatever you want, which will be provided with letters on the day without a day. Most of them are over 50 years of age, without working or teachers are expected to become professors, this is the truth of our state. This Government has not even begun to make a public administration, adequate, small and efficient reform in the service of citizens. The state is in great need of budget savings, while public debt is growing, there are many unenforceable laws.

In Kosovo it would be nice for a citizen to sit down, not to vote for such people, the state of Kosovo deserves a dignified power that works well for the citizens, where the government would be mostly 11 ministries based on the economic developments that there are also the financial capacities to maintain a small and efficient, impartial administration, with few boards and public enterprises, Kosovo needs no more than two or three public enterprises and no more than three public universities, MPs have salaries only for held sessions and abolished the absurd privileges by impoverishing citizens, ie taxpayers.

11.7.Alliance for Future of Kosovo - AAK

AAK is the centerpiece of the right-wing attempt but the leader of this party has not figured out what is a right-wing party looks like, this party has no programming links to either the right or the left in Europe country , its leader was in fact in left movement called "The People's Movement of Kosovo", but he has no knowledge of the parties and programs, even his political vocabulary does not show any program, for this party it is important to gain power, not to deal with political programs and orientations. In this party there were people who came from various parties, the party was a coalition of parties after 2012, this party suffered a major fall in its membership with the final removal of all the parties of the previous coalition such as the Parliamentary Party of Kosovo, UNIKOMB (left party), LKCK (party left), and LPK (party left). Political parties such as UNIKOMB, LKCK and LPK now do not exist, LKCK has been transformed into a new party called the Union for Movement. Another constituent subject of the AAK was the LPK - People's Movement of Kosovo.

The LPK was established as a movement of resistance, which has organized a large number of demonstrations in Western countries, and as an ultimate means of resistance was the armed struggle against the Serb occupier. In the LPK Assembly in 1993, it has also set its basic goals for war and liberation of Kosovo , so its membership has joined the KLA war, and has given the political war of the war to Kosovo's freedom. LCP is a political entity which has extended its political organization in Kosovo, and has also contributed to the establishment of AAK political coalition. LPK had given its contribution to the political organization of AAK. The role of LPK was positive and constructive during the political organization of AAK and in some political situations it was very flexible in finding political solutions within the coalition.

11.8.Parliamentary Party of Kosovo (PPK)

PPK was founded in 1991, in the spirit of the process of political pluralism, since the establishment had gathered around the intellectuals of mostly young generations and the new social structure of Kosovo. PPK's engagement was special in the then political scene in Kosovo, many political entities were established in Kosovo, what made PPK distinct from other subjects was the new spirit of the new generation that flowed as a commitment to the structure of youth, dynamism, greater enthusiasm to act quickly on the political plane. PPK was initially engaged in the activation of the peaceful -violence resistance through protests, demonstrations and general civic disobedience as a suitable form to impose a fair solution to the Kosovo issue and to prepare people for a higher degree of their own war for freedom from Serbian occupation during 1990-1999. In 1993, the PPK Steering Council decided that the party's political platform should be transformed into an active peaceful movement. PPK never ceased to have any ideas that could push forward the ideas after the arrival of Adem Demaqi at the helm of MPP, a new initiative was set up for the establishment of the Kosovo Democratic Forum, where all political parties would take part, but this forum, despite the creations, only took part in the first meeting, but other subjects were present. PPK's idea was to make a political decision-making forum to reach the goal of establishing the state of Kosovo. Later in 1997, in its program project, PPK stated that for a robberies people, what are Albanians in Kosovo, all forms of war for liberation are legitimate. PPK was a political subject that its own path of development was in its vision of political pragmatism, not in the stance, ineffectiveness and political stigma that had overtaken the political scene of Kosovo during the 1990s, political unrealism, difficult situation of the citizens of Kosovo, Serbian occupation of Kosovo was the consequence of recent events. In the development of the political and national movement PPK is committed to radical changes, while the "waiting politics" that others will create the freedom of Kosovo and independent , PPK opposes the concept of change by leading the Albanian factor. The political PPK of the Assembly of Kosovo IV in 1996 was: The necessity of movement from the country. The then political situation ultimately imposed other political behavior. Failure to concretize the political actions, and the lack of progress, the process of Kosovo's political solution at that time, prompted PPK to seek something that would be fruitful in the political arena, some political subjects were mostly passivized or in other words political exhaustion did not bring anything concrete that the process of political solution to Kosovo would begin to move. During 1996, PPK made changes to its political platform: "Domestic mobility necessity", coming to the PPK of Adem Demaq's PPK in the spirit PPK policy, began to think of new political steps that PPK had to undertake at that time, against the other political spectrum that he thought it would still be necessary to work without radical political changes identified with actions of political pacification by passive resistance. Veton Surroi was as well in period President of PPK. Bajram Kosumi ex-prime minister of Kosovo was a political leader during the 1993-1996 , and after 2000. PPK, set the political concept of active resistance which was acting during the 1990.

11.9.AQK – Alliance of Citizens of Kosovo

Was on of the founding subject of AAK, at the head of this subject was Ramush Haradinaj, the formation of the AQK was composed of several personalities and citizens of Kosovo who joined Mr. Haradinaj. The goal of Mr. Haradinaj was about to gather as many personalities around him and some who were not politically engaged in that period or earlier had been members of different parties and movements. AQK was joined by several personalities of the war and by the KPC (Kosovo Protection Corps). If we analyze a bit more about the engagement and structure of this subject in AAK, it can be said that it was a subject that was to be transitional in the full transformation of the political coalition into a single political entity, although according to the statements of some political parties in the AAK, it is stated that it was not intended for the CQK to request from the entities to join it, this subject compared to the other subjects in the KAA does not was subject to any political territorial structure the majority of the members of the AQK were only members of the AAK branches but not a territorial organization. AQK was a subject within the AAK, where his voice was strongly blamed by Ramush Haradinaj , he, Haradinaj made efforts to bring citizens and professionals (experts) and people on behalf of this subject with authority but not engaged in other current subjects. Ramush Haradinaj after taking the political leader in the coalition AAK in 2000, he had acted in opposition to the coalition's regulation that the chairman of AAK was with rotating with one year mandate , the mandate of the president was only one year, but he never respects this agreement and thus all the party in the coalition left over with the time apart from the PPK that had agreed to establish the AAK single party in the political party register, PPK left the political coalition in 2010.

12. Statute of political parties and base on law

Statutes of Political Parties

According to Law no. 03 / l-073 on General Elections in the Republic of Kosovo, respectively Article 12 which regulates the procedures to be followed by the competent authorities, in this case the Political Party Registration Office at the CEC, Article 12, Paragraph 12.3, Item f among other things, requires that political parties seeking to be enrolled in this office should have their statutes as documents that by the nature of the legal definition are known as documents binding legal obligation for the party's internal organization.

Meanwhile, according to the Rulebook from Law no. 03 / L-073 on the Registration of Political Parties, namely Article 12, which includes the framework on how and what the statute of a party should include political, it is clearly stated that the statutes of political parties should include:

(a) procedures through which citizens can become members and cease to be members of the party, as well as the rights and responsibilities of the members;

(b) the procedures to be followed for amending the party's statute or political program;

(c) the procedures to be applied by the party for its distribution, entry into the coalition electoral or union with another party;

(d) the procedures to be followed for the election of the chairman, of the members of the most senior body senior executive or other elected party officials;

(e) the procedures to be followed for the election of party candidates in the elections for The Assembly of Kosovo and the Municipal Assemblies taking into account Article 14[26];

(f) the establishment of a dispute settlement body within the Party concerned interpretation of statute;

(g) the transfer of all remaining assets after repayment of all debts on the occasion of party distribution and

(h) the duration and the rules of procedure to be applied in regular and

extraordinary members of the party, including the provision of a quorum, agenda and decision-making.

A greater role for the CEC registration office. Pursuant to the Law on General Elections in the Republic of Kosovo, respectively. Chapter III, Article 11, are sanctioned with general registration and certification provisions political subjects. This section regulates the establishment and functioning of the Office for Registration and Certification of Political Parties. The establishment and operation of the office is also envisaged by the Regulation on the Registration of Political Parties. The same provisions of general provisions that are incorporated in the aforementioned Law are also contained in this regulation. The office is

---

[26] Law of General Election

responsible for maintaining the registry of political parties, certification of all political entities that will be involved in the race for public posts and the restriction campaign expenditures and provisions for financial disclosure of this law. This office is led by the Executive Director and reports directly to the Secretariat of the CEC. Taking into account the powers of the Political Party Registration Office, it is worth it it is emphasized that the democratic performance and functioning of political parties, among others is also the responsibility of this office. Regulation for the Registration of Political Parties, except among others, clearly defines the way of electing electoral candidates. Also, an article another important thing in this Regulation is Article 17 which defines and specifies how a political party should be financed by certain individuals, party membership and by Kosovo budget. The task of the Office is to monitor the functioning of parties inbound, by observing and reporting on developments at all levels in the party. This implies the observation of elections and reporting and even sanctioning parties if they do not adhere. Their regulations and their statutes. To accomplish this task, the Office needs a number much larger staff than it is now that will be monitoring throughout Kosovo and on a longer term work of political parties and report right for all levels and for all developments.

12.1.How do political parties programs apply in to the political parties?

It is very difficult to enforce statutes and programs of political parties, moreover these programs and statutes are formal documents in order to gain the right to be registered in the capacity of a political party. Political parties in Kosovo have the Statutory Commission formally to interpret the statute of the party, but this body is a committee that advocates the political leader. Political parties in Kosovo function with a political leader, while their parties bodies are formal, internal reformation is needed for political staff establishes their own party leader.

 Party programs are not implemented at all but there is no party control mechanism or the Central Election Commission has no mandate to oversee the implementation of the statutes that have the political parties so this is just the right of the parties if they apply if they do not respond to anyone, even the political parties have their political assemblies the political leaders report based on their statutes only formally, the overall work of the political party and the financial report in most of the situations are formally apologized by party assemblies in Kosovo. There are no major debates in the

assemblies, there is not even a proper and normal debate, and everything in these party assemblies goes fast and ends within two days. The political parties in Kosovo are monopolized by the political leaders. They come out in a row and they report shortly and handshake points endorse the programs and work of party organs starting with the approval of the work of the chairman of the party and the governing board of the party. It has often happened that the members of the parties participating in the work of the party assemblies are divided unhappy and even part of the membership of a political party due to the lack of transparency in the work of the party bodies and party leader, this has happened with the LDK , where after the work of the party in this party in 2009 have departed from this party and have established the Democratic League of Dardania (LDD).

12.2.How do party bodies operate in Kosovo?

Parties organs in Kosovo function weakly or far, or more formally because the parties has a political leader as in the former communist era of Kosovo. These parties leaders in Kosovo make all decisions and have little or no affiliation within the party , who may be against it may even leave the party by the leader. Parties organs have problems with making independent decisions based on the Statute of the party such as PDK, LDK, AAK, NISMA Social Democrats. Parties organs do not match in it is in harmony with the interests of the broad anarchy that have but act based on the decisions of the leader. It has also happened that in these parties also leave all the individuals if they have different opinions with the leader such as AAK. Parties organs are not respected by the leader at all, the party in Kosovo acts formally with acts as the statute they have, there has never been for political parties to establish party bodies as a party assembly or leadership as more responsible bodies for politics and membership. In LDK there were two or three of them involved in the negotiations for the establishment of a coalition to lead the government, in AAK only the party leader, PDK only Hashim Thaci and later only Kadri Veseli has decided for coalitions. These parties do not even have transparency before the citizens and their membership, political actions are not clear and very little information is given to members of their parties about political decisions. This also happens with running for MPs in the political party in Kosovo, as well as appointing people in the post of minister or The Kosovo Assembly. Leaders are also involved in employment in public institutions of members of their families, party people throughout the although legally the boards are professional and not political.

12.4. The President of political party

The party leader in most of the political parties in Kosovo is the only one and final person to make decisions within the party. The party leader decided who is person to run for potential deputies in central elections at the local level, even some time did not allow the party's own branches to make proposals for mayor or branch president. The president has a reserved power. Kosovo works with a political leader, the parties have no internal democracy, the mayor almost always decides to nominate ministers in the government, leaders are always candidates for Prime Minister (PDK, AAK, with liberal are LDK). The chairman has an authoritarian power and is often the biggest obstacle to democratizing the party, the leader also decides who will be his foe, chiefly not an influential adviser to party chairpersons but has only a formal advisor and often does not have to become a counselor. The leader seems to be someone who cannot stand by the members of the party bodies by the Steering Council or the Presidency of the Party. The president often does not accept advice from anyone in Kosovo, he or she directs the party and if he has a high position in the state for all, for example, Hashim Thaci decides for the dialogue and there is no expert engaged in dialogue with Serbia for normalization of relations between the two states. Thaci seems to be the only influential and decisive figure in Kosovo politics; he is also the only person who decides to accept the embargoes or not their admission in Brussels. Thaci is the most criticized person in Kosovo for the agreement that Kosovo should have representations in footnote in international meeting. He is not more political leader who was once the founder of the PDK, but in silence it is still a president of the party, that he still has a party in his hand , despite being a president and with the Constitution of the Republic of Kosovo he cannot be included in party politics formally , he has resigned in formal manner from his former party, to take the position of the President of the State of Kosovo. He has never been admitted to being a mayor who has a unifying role in the political spectrum, he has lost trust in the party, he is not respectful of the opposition party for the role of the president of the state. Hashim Thaci presents himself as a leader in Kosovo's liberation and as a politician declare independent of Kosovo state from Serbia, but in the peace hero for a normalization of relations with Serbia. Thaci is criticized for the agreement on an ethnic Serb assembly within Kosovo's territory. It is said that with the agreement on Association of Serbian Municipalities has made an ineffective deal for Kosovo these critiques come without stop from the opposition (VV, LDK, PSD). Even AAK leader Ramush Haradinaj is evaluated to have an authoritarian power within his party, he has issued almost all decisions for ministerial posts, for deputies, for drafting a list for deputy for the regional elections, co-operation with party leader is more he has never held a proper attitude to his anarchy and party organs, he has divided his political party into two parts, a large number of important people since the establishment have left the Haradinaj party, often did many criticisms for members of his party because is not collaborating with experts, and having problems with his school education and overall preparation in the quality of the political leader. Isa Mustafa remains a person who had come to the post of party chairman, dismissing former LDK leader Fatmir Sejdiu, who violated the Constitution of Kosovo, which had two seats and that the constitution of the state of Kosovo forbade the chairman's state and the head of a political party. LDK leader Ibrahim Rugova has the most powerful respectability in his party, he was unity in his party,and he was almost the same as Thaci and Haradinaj. For all party situations he was a last a nd final person who made he final decision, he had given the post of Prime Minister Ramush Haradinaj even though he had led a small party with only 9%, he as a president was quietly criticized within LDK, but no one in the LDK had come against Haradinaj, in LDK for forgetting the post of prime minister Ibrahim Rugova had done.

2. Presidency of the party

The party leadership in Kosovo was supposed to serve as the executive body of party bodies such as the Assembly and the General Council or the Steering Council, but the leadership is often formal and with the aim of not having the capability of this party body, the leaders have increased the number of members of the board making it impossible to decide or enforce decisions of the Assembly of the Party or of the Governing Board or the General Assembly. That is why the leadership of a party in Kosovo consists of 53 members (PDK), AAK up to 76 members of the Presidency, LDK 33 members; some parties have a mix of competencies between party bodies such as the Chairperson and the Steering Council. The Presidency is prevented from being active in decision-making and voting, because this is impossible for the political leader who holds all the decision-making power for himself and is the person who always decides on the party. Until now the party is neither transparent in this direction nor for the this decision-making of party presidencies. Political parties in Kosovo act in accordance with the demands of the leader, almost the entire body is in support of political leaders, so far no such body has publicly appeared in the media that it has decided to enter one of the parties in the coalition. The statute clearly states that decisions need to be made in accordance with the will of their members. The party presidency must be a party-executive body of strategic policies that sets the Steering Council and long-term visionary politics set by the party's governing council. But this does not happen or does not happen very rarely, so far these bodies have formally acted, party spokesman very little used by the political party in Kosovo more individuals emerge and represent their parties in the debates sometimes without even the attitude of a party to send them into political debate, come out in the media to give their views more than party attitudes or party decisions.

3. The General Council of the political parties

The Steering Council or the general is a decision-making body in some political parties based on the party statutes as the LDK example, political parties based on their statutes every four years should have electoral assemblies based also on the requirements of CEC regulations, Kosovo still there is no law for political parties.

CHAPTER TWO

Political Parties in Macedonia

The critical players to consider in Macedonian politics are the political parties, which control much of Macedonian political life, both national and local. Conservative political party structures dominate the political arena. Male-dominated, hierarchical, centralized, and with closed processes, they perpetuate those in power. Much of their politicking, building alliances, and taking decisions takes place at times and in locations where women are not comfortable or welcome. Organizational procedures are not transparent, participatory, and democratic[27].

Political parties include the Democratic Alternative (DA), the Democratic Party of Albanians (DPA), the Liberal Democratic Party (LDP), the Liberal Party (LP), the Party of Democratic Prosperity (PDP), the Social Democratic Union of Macedonia (SDSM), the Internal Macedonian Revolutionary Organization - Democratic Party for Macedonian National Unity (VMRO-DPMNE), and the Internal Macedonian Revolutionary Organization True Macedonian Reformist Option (VMRO- VMRO). Although political parties are brimming with structure, rules, and regulations, very few of these procedures are followed. Although all parties claim to have a well-defined place along the political spectrum and to subscribe to a particular ideology, power and greater role than ideology, and that parties revolve around the personalities of their leaders. A small cadre at the top of each party decides who will serve in certain positions within the party or the government, determines policy, and develops party platforms. The political parties are highly centralized, information is rarely communicated downwards, not even to party members, and true competition for voters does not exist. Most citizens view political parties as organizations aimed at obtaining or maintaining power so that the party leaders and their faithful can reap both political and

---

[27] Macedonia - Political Parties, https://www.globalsecurity.org/military/world/europe/mk-politics-parties.htm,25.05.2018

economic rewards. Consequently, public esteem for political parties is very low. Macedonia's traditionally pro-Yugoslav stance permitted the Social Democratic Union of Macedonia (SDSM) – the chief successor to the League of Communists which ruled the republic during Tito's Yugoslavia – to remain in power through a governing coalition which followed the first multi-party elections in November 1990. At the same time, the Macedonian people's own strain of nationalism was reflected in the founding and general popularity of the Internal Macedonian Revolutionary Organization ("VMRO," which was also the name of a 19th century extremist Macedonian liberation group), which, in fact, won more votes in the 1990 elections than any other single political party. Similarly, the many other ethnic groups comprising Macedonia's population formed their own, ethnically based parties. This included the sizable Albanian community – which comprises at least one-quarter of the country's population – as well as the smaller but still significant Roma, Serb and Turkish communities[28]. The leading ethnically Albanian political party – the Party for Democratic Prosperity (PDP) – was invited into the governing coalition, and a prominent politician from the Tito era, Kiro Gligorov, was chosen to serve as President of the Republic[29].

Although of a more tolerant, reformed communist tradition, those who governed Macedonia as a result of the 1990 elections lacked strong democratic inclinations, while preoccupation with the external situation post- poned serious consideration of domestic reforms. Thus, when parliamentary and presidential elections were held in October 1994, many of the same electoral problems from 1990 – voter registration lists, media bias and badly apportioned electoral districts – still existed, albeit not to such significant degrees that the outcome was brought into question by international observers[30]. Moreover, by that time strains between the Albanian and Macedonian communities became more pronounced, with the founding of ethnically Albanian political parties like the Party for Democratic Prosperity of Albanians (PDPA) which were decidedly more separatist in their inclinations. The still nationalist VMRO-DPMNE (the additional initials standing for the

---

[28] Macedonia - Political Parties, https://www.globalsecurity.org/military/world/europe/mk-politics-parties.htm,25.05.2018
[29] Macedonia - Political Parties, https://www.globalsecurity.org/military/world/europe/mk-politics-parties.htm,25.05.2018
[30] Macedonia - Political Parties, https://www.globalsecurity.org/military/world/europe/mk-politics-parties.htm,25.05.2018

"Democratic Party of Macedonian Unity" following splits in the original party) enlisted the support of some other parties in attempting to deny the elections any legitimacy by boycotting the second round. The ruling SDSM nevertheless was able to retain power, and Kiro Gligorov won a five-year term in the first directly elected presidential race.

On 31 October 1999, Macedonian voters went to the polls to choose a new president. Six candidates ran in the election. Originally, the VMRO-DPMNE coalition with the DA was based on the assumption that Ljupco Georgievski of the former would become prime minister with a victory in 1998 while the DA's Vasil Tupurkovski of the latter would be the coalition's candidate for president[31]. After months of haggling, however, VMRO-DPMNE decided to field its own presidential candidate, Boris Trajkovski, who had come to political prominence as a Deputy Foreign Minister during the Kosovo crisis[32]. Tupurkovski ran as the candidate of the Democratic Alliance alone. The SDSM, now in the opposition, chose Tito Petkovski, who had been the President of the unicameral Macedonian Assembly prior to the 1998 elections, as its nominee. Stojan Andov, who preceded Petkovski as Assembly President prior to his party's break with an earlier SDSM coalition, was the candidate of the Liberal Democratic Party (LDP) which formed in 1997 from two other parties emerging from more reformist wing of the former League of Communists[33]. Democratic Party of Albanians (DPA), a governing coalition partner, nominated Muharem Nexhipi as its candidate while the PDP nominated Muhamed Halili to vie for the votes within the ethnic Albanian community. This community, in fact, represents almost an entirely separate polity in Macedonia, yet the participation of the two candidates indicated a willingness of the community to consider the head of state their representative and not that solely of those of Macedonian nationality[34].

The inability of any of them to win a majority of the votes cast required a second round on November 14 between the top two vote-getters.

---

[31] Macedonia - Political Parties, https://www.globalsecurity.org/military/world/europe/mk-politics-parties.htm,25.05.2018

[32] Macedonia - Political Parties, https://www.globalsecurity.org/military/world/europe/mk-politics-parties.htm,25.05.2018

[33] Macedonia - Political Parties, https://www.globalsecurity.org/military/world/europe/mk-politics-parties.htm,25.05.2018

[34] Macedonia - Political Parties, https://www.globalsecurity.org/military/world/europe/mk-politics-parties.htm,25.05.2018

Boris Trajkovski of the ruling Internal Macedonian Revolutionary Organization – Democratic Party for Macedonian Unity (VMRO-DPMNE) edged out his opponent, Tito Petkovski, of the opposition Social Democratic Union of Macedonia (SDSM), although irregularities forced second-round reruns on December 5 and were used by Petkovski supporters as a pretext for questioning the integrity of the result[35]. On 24 November 2000, the Democratic Alternative (DA) announced that it would leave the governing coalition to join the Social Democratic Union of Macedonia (SDSM) in a bid to form a new government coalition. This move came after Prime Minister Ljubco Georgievski fired prominent DA cabinet minister Melodic as a final message that the DA was no longer a welcome nor necessary partner in the governing coalition with VMRO-DPMNE. In a joint press conference with VRMO-VMRO, PDP and SDSM, DA announced its support of its new coalition partners. SDSM announced that it would be pursuing a vote of no confidence against the governing coalition[36]. Shortly thereafter, Savo Klimovski, president of the parliament and a member of DA, was forced to resign. For SDSM to be successful in ousting the present government, all of DA and the majority of PDP would have to support it. During subsequent votes in parliament, more than half of the PDP members supported the governing coalition, causing SDSM's bid for a change in government to fail[37].

The outcome of these political maneuverings strengthened the position of the governing VMRO-DPMNE, as opposed to bringing the government down. The government appeared to have the support of 75 deputies, an increase of 8 from when VMRO-DPMNE was partnered with DA. By moving quickly to install the new cabinet ministers from the Liberals and the PDP, VMRO-DPMNE has ensured a stable government. The appointment of six Liberal Party (LP) deputy ministers has guaranteed the support of that party, and there does not seem to be an immediate threat of a vote of no confidence[38].

---

[35] Macedonia - Political Parties, https://www.globalsecurity.org/military/world/europe/mk-politics-parties.htm,25.05.2018

[36] Macedonia - Political Parties, https://www.globalsecurity.org/military/world/europe/mk-politics-parties.htm,25.05.2018

[37] Macedonia - Political Parties, https://www.globalsecurity.org/military/world/europe/mk-politics-parties.htm,25.05.2018

[38] Macedonia - Political Parties, https://www.globalsecurity.org/military/world/europe/mk-politics-parties.htm,25.05.2018

Key Political Parties in Albania

After the January 21 riots and a prolonged power struggle that has hampered its EU aspirations and strained the country's fragile institutions, Albania's political parties head to the May 8 local elections, considered as key to the country's democratic credentials.

Democratic Party, PD

The Democratic Party of Albania is a Centre-right political organization and the main governing party since 2005. It is an observer member of the European People's Party, EPP, the European umbrella for Centre-right parties, and a full member of the Centrist Democrat International[39]. The party was founded in 1991 following student demonstrations that brought down the communist regime and was the first opposition party to be formed after the fall of the one-party system. The party has been controlled since 1991 by Albania's current Prime Minister, Sali Berisha.

PD first took power in 1992 after winning the general election under the leadership of Berisha and Aleksander Meksi who governed as president and prime minister. They lost power in 1997 when snap elections were called to pacify a civil unrest that broke out following the bankruptcy of a series of pyramid-style investment schemes. In the 2001 elections, the party received 37.1 per cent of the vote and gained 46 of the 140 seats in parliament. In the July 2005 parliamentary elections, the Democratic Party won 56 of the 140 seats and its allies won 18. A coalition it had built with several minor parties won a majority of 70 seats in the 140-member parliament in the 2009 election, with PD itself winning 40. 2 percent of the popular vote and 68 seats[40].

Socialist Party, PS

The Socialist Party of Albania, a centre-left, social democratic party, is currently the leading opposition party in the country with 65 of the 140 seats in parliament. The Socialists first took power in 1997 following the unrest over the collapse of the pyramid-style funds. It won again four

---

[39] Key Political Parties in Albania, http://www.balkaninsight.com/en/article/who-is-who-political-parties-in-albania

[40] Key Political Parties in Albania, http://www.balkaninsight.com/en/article/who-is-who-political-parties-in-albania

years later with 73 seats in parliament, enabling it to form the government[41].In the July 2005 general election, the Socialist Party lost its majority and the Democratic Party of Sali Berisha took over, heading a centre-right coalition. In the June 2009 elections, it won 65 seats in Parliament. The Socialist Party of Albania is the legal successor to the Party of Labour of Albania, PLA, which was once the Communist Party of Albania.It was formed after the dissolution of the Albanian Labour Party at the Tenth Congress of the party in June 1991[42]. Fatos Nano, a reform Communist, was elected first chairman. Nano controlled the party until 2005 when he resigned following the election defeat that year, and was succeeded by Tirana mayor Edi Rama. The party is a member of Socialist International[43].

Socialist Movement for Integration, LSI

Formed in 2004 as a splinter group of the Socialist Party of Albania, PS, the Socialist Movement for Integration, joined the Democratic Party in a coalition after the 2009 general elections. LSI won four seats in Parliament after the June 2009 election, down one from the previous poll in 2005, but it holds several key government posts including the Minister of Foreign Affairs, the Minister of Economy and that of Health as the main junior partner in the government of Prime Minister Sali Berisha. Purportedly a Centre-left political group, the LSI is gathered around the strong personality of its party boss Ilir Meta. However, the party has been swept recently by allegations of corruption, following the indictment of Meta and former Minister of Economy Dritan Prifti on corruption charges. The indictments follow the publication of a video tape in January, where Meta then deputy prime minister and Prifti are heard discussing alleged corrupt deals. Both Prifti and Meta have denied any wrongdoing[44].

---

[41] Key Political Parties in Albania, http://www.balkaninsight.com/en/article/who-is-who-political-parties-in-albania

[42] Key Political Parties in Albania, http://www.balkaninsight.com/en/article/who-is-who-political-parties-in-albania

[43] Key Political Parties in Albania, http://www.balkaninsight.com/en/article/who-is-who-political-parties-in-albania

[44] Key Political Parties in Albania, http://www.balkaninsight.com/en/article/who-is-who-political-parties-in-albania

Montenegro: Key Political Parties

The Democratic Party of Socialists, DPS

The governing party in Montenegro for over two decades, the leader of the DPS is Milo Djukanovic, the party chief since 1998, who quit as Prime Minister in 2010. Other key members are the President of Montenegro, Filip Vujanovic, who is the party's vice-president and the former head of the State Union Serbia and Montenegro, Svetozar Marovic. Another key figure is the Mayor of Podgorica, Miomir Mugosa.

The DPS holds 36 of the 81 seats in the parliament, the Skupstina. The party is the successor party to the League of Communists of Montenegro, which wound up in 1991, adopting a new name and constitution.

The DPS has won every general election in Montenegro since the first multi-party elections of 1990. Initially, the DPS favoured maintaining the loose "State Union" with Serbia. In the early 1990s, the party was close to the Serbian nationalist regime in Belgrade of Slobodan Milosevic. But in 1997, a section of the party under Djukanovic began turning against Milosevic and towards the idea of reestablishing Montenegro's independence. The pro-Serbian, pro-Milosevic element then broke away in 1998 to form a new party, the Socialist People's Party. The DPS was the main political force behind the successful pro-independence referendum held in 2006.Today the party presents itself as the main advocate of EU membership and the attainment of European standards in all areas of the economy and society. In June 2012, the DPS-led government celebrated the official start of membership talks with the EU.For its part, the EU has told Montenegro to curb corruption and organized crime if it is serious about closing negotiations. The DPS also strongly favours joining NATO, despite the lack of popular support for this idea. Nominally a social democrat party and a member of Socialist International, opposition parties accuse it of pursuing neoliberal economic policies and of disregarding welfare safeguards. It is one of the best organized parties in the region, if not in Europe, with approximately 100,000 members, more than fifth of the total number of registered voters in the country. Despite the existence of ethnic minority parties in Montenegro, many members of those minorities, such as Bosniaks and Albanians, prefer to vote for the DPS.In the current government, the Croatian Citizen Initiative, HGI, and the Bosniak Party, BS, are coalition partners along with the Social Democrat Party, SDP. In the upcoming election on October 14, 2012, the DPS will run together with the SDP and Liberal Party, LP, which failed to enter the parliament in 2009 election.

The Social Democrat Party, SDP

A relatively small party, the Social Democrats have often held an important role in politics as a coalition partner of the DPS, enabling the larger party to form a majority government. They hold nine of the 81 seats in parliament, following the 2009 parliamentary elections. Together with the DPS, the party was among the main advocates of Montenegro's renewed independence. The party's president, also now the speaker of parliament, Ranko Krivokapic, had the honour of officially proclaiming Montenegro's independence on May 22, 2006. The party was formed in the early Nineties as a union of several parties of a social democrat and socialist coloration.

In the first multi-party election of 1990 they affiliated with the Alliance of Reform Forces of Yugoslavia, led by Yugoslavia's reformist prime minister, Ante Markovic. During the Yugoslav wars the party was known for its anti-war stance. Today, party officials are often accused of nepotism by the opposition media. Although it has been in coalition with the DPS at national level since 1998, the SDP sporadically criticizes DPS policies, especially when it comes to the economy and privatization of former industrial giants. In several local elections over the past years, it has run independently. One of the highest profile local disputes with the DPS was in the capital, Podgorica, which resulted in the break-up of their coalition in the municipal assembly in 2011. Ahead of the 2012 general election, the party stated that it might run independently, but in July it agreed to form another pre-electoral coalition with the DPS[45].

The Socialist People's Party, SNP

The main opposition party in Montenegro holds 16 of the 81 seats in parliament[46]. The SNP was founded in 1997 by the pro-Serbian wing of

---

[45] Montenegro Kay Political Parties
http://www.balkaninsight.com/en/article/montenegro-key-political-parties
[46] Montenegro Kay Political Parties
http://www.balkaninsight.com/en/article/montenegro-key-political-parties

the DPS and was the leading force in the bloc supporting the continued "State Union" with Serbia in the independence referendum of May 2006.

After the bloc lost the referendum, the SNP suffered a loss of support as a result of which the party's president, Predrag Bulatovic, resigned[47].

The new leader, Srdjan Milic, reformed the party. Under his guidance, the SNP moved away from concentrating on the relationship with Serbia and adopted a more civic, social democratic, pro-European agenda[48].

This change in emphasis shored up the SNP's voting bloc and helped it to emerge as the second-largest party in the 2009 elections, after the DPS.

Over the last government's term, the SNP softened its rhetoric towards the ruling DPS, which some interpreted as a sign that the party might be seeking better ties with the DPS[49].

There was speculation that two wings were emerging within the party, one led by its former leader, Bulatovic, and the other by Milic[50].

After the formation in July 2012 of the Democratic Front, an opposition political coalition initiated by the two other significant opposition parties, the Movement for Changes and New Serbian Democracy, the existence of factions within the party was confirmed[51].

Bulatovic and many other senior party members joined the Democratic Front in August 2012. By doing so, they automatically dismissed themselves from the SNP because they had acted contrary to the official

---

[47] Montenegro Kay Political Parties
http://www.balkaninsight.com/en/article/montenegro-key-political-parties
[48] Montenegro Kay Political Parties
http://www.balkaninsight.com/en/article/montenegro-key-political-parties

[49] Montenegro Kay Political Parties
http://www.balkaninsight.com/en/article/montenegro-key-political-parties
[50] Montenegro Kay Political Parties
http://www.balkaninsight.com/en/article/montenegro-key-political-parties
[51] Montenegro Kay Political Parties
http://www.balkaninsight.com/en/article/montenegro-key-political-parties

party policy, the party having not agreed coalition terms with the Front[52].

Milic and the rest of the party's leadership, on the other hand, have decided to run in the 2012 election independently, although they do not reject the possibility of forming a post-electoral coalition with the Democratic Front[53].

The Democratic Front:

The Democratic Front was established in July 2012 with the aim of replacing the regime of the Democratic Party of Socialists, DPS, which it describes as "authoritarian, retrograde, criminalistics and oligarchic"[54].

A broad coalition, it was established by the two opposition parties, New Serbian Democracy, NOVA, and Movement for Changes, PzP. Later a number of independent intellectuals, civil society leaders as well as a wing of Socialist People's Party joined. It is headed by Miodrag Lekic, a former Yugoslav and Montenegrin ambassador to several countries and Montenegro's foreign minister from 1992 to 1995[55].

Although its leaders have appealed to all who feel dissatisfied with the current government, the Front has not attracted many ethnic minority Bosniaks or Albanian members[56]. The Front has partly adopted the rhetoric of the civic protests that took place in the capital in 2012. It demands the investigation of dubious privatizations and the termination of certain investment contracts that it deems harmful to the economy[57]. It also demands the start of a lustration process[58]. Those

---

[52] Montenegro Kay Political Parties
http://www.balkaninsight.com/en/article/montenegro-key-political-parties
[53] Montenegro Kay Political Parties
http://www.balkaninsight.com/en/article/montenegro-key-political-parties
[54] Montenegro Kay Political Parties
http://www.balkaninsight.com/en/article/montenegro-key-political-parties

[55] Montenegro Kay Political Parties
http://www.balkaninsight.com/en/article/montenegro-key-political-parties
[56] Montenegro Kay Political Parties
http://www.balkaninsight.com/en/article/montenegro-key-political-parties
[57] Montenegro Kay Political Parties
http://www.balkaninsight.com/en/article/montenegro-key-political-parties
[58] Montenegro Kay Political Parties
http://www.balkaninsight.com/en/article/montenegro-key-political-parties

involved in corruption and criminal structures must be put on trial. Its political program comprises a list of 595 proposals. It holds that the metal industry should be basis of the real economy and that tourism needs further development. It says it will achieve the reconciliation of the country's deeply polarized society[59].

The Front's symbol, written in both Cyrillic and Latin alphabets, portray a dove with an olive tree and combine old and new Montenegrin flags. The Front is pro-European Union, but says that the question of joining NATO should be put to a referendum[60].

The Movement For Changes, PZP

A pro-European party founded in 2006 from a civic NGO, the party is distinguished by its passionate opposition to the DPS. Defeat of the government is its cherished goal. The PZP held a neutral position in the 2006 independence referendum. Since then, it has maintained that while it favoured independence in 2006 it did not want to be part of an alliance led by Djukanovic. Although it started well for a new party, winning 11 seats in the 2006 elections, in 2009 it fell back to only five[61].

The loss was attributed to voter confusion over its choice of allies and partners. Its coalition with the DPS when the party was part of the two-thirds-majority vote needed for the adoption of the new constitution in 2007 alienated most other opposition parties. They voted against the constitution (Serbian List, SNP, People's Party, and Democratic Serbian Party). The DPS, PzP, the Liberal Party and the BS, on the other hand, voted in favour[62].

After this brief alignment with the ruling parties, the PzP went back to fiercely opposing the government, and, over time, established close

---

[59] Montenegro Kay Political Parties
http://www.balkaninsight.com/en/article/montenegro-key-political-parties
[60] Montenegro Kay Political Parties
http://www.balkaninsight.com/en/article/montenegro-key-political-parties

[61] Montenegro Kay Political Parties
http://www.balkaninsight.com/en/article/montenegro-key-political-parties
[62] Montenegro Kay Political Parties
http://www.balkaninsight.com/en/article/montenegro-key-political-parties

cooperation with New Serbian Democracy, NOVA, even at the expense of some policy choices it previously advocated. For example, although it voted for the constitution, which stipulated Montenegrin as an official language, the PzP later supported other opposition parties in seeking improved status for the Serbian language[63]. This won it back some support among pro-Serbian voters, but the presence of party members at an opposition rally against Kosovo's independence in October 2008 alienated ethnic Albanians. The PzP's close cooperation with NOVA became more stable in 2012, with the formation of the Democratic Front, a broad coalition. But critics of the party say that it only wants to participate in the Front to protect itself from a major electoral defeat. The party leader, Nebojsa Medojevic, ran for the presidency in 2008, coming third with 17 per cent of the votes[64].

Positive Montenegro, PCG:

One of the newest parties in the country, it was formed in May 2012 under the leadership of former green activist Darko Pajovic with the aim of showcasing new people and ideas. Positive Montenegro presents itself as a new, civic, Centre-left force with a "clean past". It aims to focus on socio-economic issues. It also aims for a more moderate rhetoric than some of the older parties, like the Movement for Changes, PzP, and it steers clear of quarrels over issues of national identity.The party advocates a socially responsible state, arguing for tight controls of natural resources and help for those who are struggling with the market economy. It will run independently in the 2012 election, and opinion polls indicate that it is likely to gain enough votes to enter parliament.

The Bosniak Party, BS

Founded in 2006 to protect the interests of the Bosniak [Muslim] minority, which makes up 7.7 per cent of the population, according to the 2003 census, it was formed out of a merger of four small parties: the International Democratic Union, the Party For Democratic Action, the

---

[63] Montenegro Kay Political Parties
http://www.balkaninsight.com/en/article/montenegro-key-political-parties
[64] Montenegro Kay Political Parties
http://www.balkaninsight.com/en/article/montenegro-key-political-parties

Democratic Alliance of Bosniaks and the Party of National Equality. The party lent the DPS-led government significant support in the independence referendum of 2006. Since the Bosniak minority is concentrated in certain areas of the country, the party favours devolving powers to regions.The BS has decided to run in the 2012 general election independently.

The Democratic Union of Albanians, DUA

Led by Ferhat Dinosa, it is one of four parties that aim to protect the rights of the ethnic Albanian minority, which makes up 5 per cent of the population, according to the 2003 census. It has one seat in parliament. The other three parties are Forca, the Democratic League of Montenegro and the Albanian Alternative. Each also has one seat in parliament.

Political parties in Serbia

Serbian party

 Politics in Serbia after 2000 has been dominated by two large and fairly polarized parties. On the one hand, there is the pro-European DS, which has been the main protagonist of the 2000 revolution and standing the prime minister from 2000-2004 and from 2008 on[65]. On the other extreme, the SRS has over long periods been Serbia's largest party, replacing the Socialists as the main player of the old regime forces since 2003[66]. Besides these two poles, the DSS could not only profit from the DS' electoral weakness in the parliamentary elections 2003, but as well over large periods hold the quite comfortable position of the kingmaker in the median of the political spectrum; none of the political option could for a majority without the DSS' support[67]. This helped the DSS, even if increasingly losing votes, to lead coalition governments from 2004 until 2008. Political parties in Serbia give

---

[65] Political parties in Serbiahttps: //www. bochsler. eu/publi/ bochsler_serbiacountry.pdf

[66]Serbian Parties, https://www.bochsler.eu/publi/bochsler_serbiacountry.pdf
Political parties in Serbia, https://www.bochsler.eu/publi/bochsler_serbiacountry.pdf
https://www.bochsler.eu/publi/bochsler_serbiacountry.pdf

[67] Serbian Parties, https://www.bochsler.eu/publi/bochsler_serbiacountry.pdf
Political parties in Serbia, https://www.bochsler.eu/publi/bochsler_serbiacountry.pdf
https://www.bochsler.eu/publi/bochsler_serbiacountry.pdf

wide powers to the party presidency, and in many cases, their powers have been more and more increased over time. In the case of the SRS, the party organs appear as fairly marginal compared to the extended presidential strength, including the interpretation of the party program and policy decisions, the nomination and dismissal of the general secretary and the four deputy presidents. Similarly, the president of the SPO, after the reform of the party statute in 1998, was empowered to nominate the party presidency and a third of the members of the party's executive committee. Exceptions are only the SPS and the G17+, whose presidents have mainly the role of the party coordinator and representative (Goati, 2004: 127-130)[68]. The strong position of the party leadership emanates however not only from the parties' own statutes, that have but as well to the electoral system and the practiced system of resignation in the Serbian parliament[69]. The party can decide on its own, and after the elections, on the composition of the parliamentary delegation[70]. This does enable the party leaderships not only to nominate deputes that were not competing in the elections, and to punish disliked candidates. Furthermore, several parties ask their deputies for blank declarations of resignation, that they might use against the members of their parliamentary group, namely if they should decide to switch the party. Such practice is however better understandable, if accounting that party switches are very common in post-communist legislatures, and in Serbia too (Orlović, 2006: 110-114)[71].

Democratic Party (DS) After 1989, the Democratic Party was the first opposition party in Serbia, and until the Socialists' trajectory, leading to a formation of a common governmental coalition after the 2008 elections, the party was always one of the main opponents of the Socialists. The DS leader Zoran Đinđić was one of the most prominent figures of the Serbian opposition all over the 1990s, and the party one of the key player of the 2000 revolution and the single largest member

---

[68] Political parties in Serbiahttps://www.bochsler.eu/publi/bochsler_serbiacountry.pdf

[69] Political parties in Serbia, https://www.bochsler.eu/publi/bochsler_serbiacountry.pdf
Political parties in Serbia, https://www.bochsler.eu/publi/bochsler_serbiacountry.pdf
https://www.bochsler.eu/publi/bochsler_serbiacountry.pdf

[70]Political parties in Serbia, https://www.bochsler.eu/publi/bochsler_serbiacountry.pdf
https://www.bochsler.eu/publi/bochsler_serbiacountry.pdf

[71] Political parties in Serbia, https://www.bochsler.eu/publi/bochsler_serbiacountry.pdf
https://www.bochsler.eu/publi/bochsler_serbiacountry.pdf

of the DOS opposition coalition[72]. After having served as prime minister since 2000, Đinđić was assassinated in office in March 2003, and became a symbol for the new liberal period afterwards, for democratic and economic reforms, and for leading Serbia towards the European Union. Locating the DS solely at the anti-nationalist pole would be misleading; in certain periods in the 1990s, the party devoted its policy clearly to the national project of Greater Serbia, namely calling for a tearing up of Bosnia and Herzegovina in 1994 and 1995, and the creation of an independent Serbian Republic there (Goati, 2004: 41). Đinđić's successor in party office Boris Tadić, was rather following a conciliating course of compromises with the national-conservative parties[73]. This goes in line with the new role of the party in the institutional system[74]. As of 2004, it held the presidential office with Boris Tadić, and needed first to cooperate with a government coalition lead by the nationalist-conservative DSS, and was later (2007-2008) included in a DSS-lead cabinet. In the period until 2007, prime minister Koštunica (DSS) was perceived to have substantial influence over Tadić. Examples for the appeasing course of the DS with the nationalists are the DS' approval for an important role of the Serbian Orthodox church in the state (Gajić, 2005), Tadić's only half-hearted excuses for Serbian mass crimes,12 or his radical rhetoric on the Kosovo issue for the domestic public, namely a symbolic visit to the Kosovo Serbs in March 2005.13 One of the possibly most painful flirts with the nationalists and the suspected opinion of the majority was the DS' support for the new Serbian constitution in the 2006 referendum. In economic terms, DS favours liberal reforms, while promising socially egalitarian policies (Stojiljković, 2007a: 144-145). Under the leadership of Zoran Đinđić and the interim prime minister after the Đinđić murder, Zoran Živković, the willingness for fast reforms has been more pronounced than in the Tadić period. The party advocates civic rights and minority rights, and has expressed its willingness to support a strong autonomy for Vojvodina. After 2006, the DS made several policy moves and created symbolic events in order to re-

---

[72] Political parties in Serbia, https://www.bochsler.eu/publi/bochsler_serbiacountry.pdf
https://www.bochsler.eu/publi/bochsler_serbiacountry.pdf

[73] Political parties in Serbia, https://www.bochsler.eu/publi/bochsler_serbiacountry.pdf
https://www.bochsler.eu/publi/bochsler_serbiacountry.pdf

[74] Political Parties in Serbia, https://www.bochsler.eu/publi/bochsler_serbiacountry.pdf
https://www.bochsler.eu/publi/bochsler_serbiacountry.pdf

position itself as a pronounced pro-reformist force, and not to leave this field to the new entering LDP that positioned close to the DS with a more decided pro-reform direction. In the 2007 elections, the DS tried to attach to the legacy of Đinđić, calling for the renaming of a Belgrade boulevard after the murdered prime minister, and putting his widow Ružica Đinđić on top of its electoral list (although she did not enter the DS parliamentary delegation after the elections). In terms of its program, the DS emphasised its reform credibility through the nomination of Božidar Đelić as prime ministerial candidate, finance minister in the Đinđić government and is seen as being committed to drastic economic reforms.14 The pro-European and reformist credentials of the DS were underlined by the visit of the EU enlargement commissar Oliver Rehn to president Boris Tadić in the last days of the campaign.

Liberal-Democratic Party (LDP) With the Liberal-Democratic party, a new pro-reform player has emerged, five years after the start of Serbia's transition. The creation and positioning of the party can only be understood if looking at the large pro-reform party, the DS. The DS membership was always pronouncedly pro-European and pro-reform, but as one of the largest party, it was after 2000 in several periods in different roles in governmental responsibility, and was partly behaving pragmatically. After the Đinđić murder, the circle of persons around Đinđić was replaced by different party streams, Boris Tadić became party president in February 2004, and the DS moved towards a pragmatic cooperation with the DSS. This grew dissatisfaction in the most reformist wing of the party. On the 2004 DS party congress, Čedomir Jovanović, deputy prime minister in the interim government in 2003, attacked the DS leadership for the cooperation with prime minister Koštunica, whom he intituled the "new Milošević". In the aftermath, a group around Jovanović tried to form the Liberal-Democratic Fraction inside the DS. The DS, however, excluded Jovanović for this attempt (cf. Goati, 2006: 172), and he in turn founded the new LDP on 5 November 2005. The party attempts to be seen as the only guarantee for a continuation of the Đinđić reform program, accusing the DS that it stalled its pro-European reform program. Accordingly, reforms and change is the first priority in the party program,15 and a solution to the questions of The Hague and Kosovo – problems inherited from the Milošević regime – figure among the first points on this way of reforms and European integration. The party argues that Serbia needs to face its recent past, and deal with war crimes committed in the 1990s, as a basis of societal modernization. Issues such as lustration, human rights, autonomy for multi-cultural regions, and Western integration (into EU, NATO, but as well through increased cooperation with neighboring states) take an important place in the program. With regards to economic issues, the party takes clearly liberal-conservative stands, and wants to reduce the size of the government. The party favors an acceleration of the transition, increased efforts in privatization, the transfer of state regulatory activities on independent, market oriented regulatory bodies, and the abolishment of state-controlled prices, which should lead to economic growth and reduce poverty. With regards to social welfare, the party favors a reform of the Serbian education system, wants to replace the state-controlled health care with a mandatory health insurance, and under the title "social policies", the program speaks of equal chances instead of criminal networks, client-orientation, increased quality, efficacy and instead of linear social subsidies. For the fight against poverty, the party does not list redistributive programs, but rather accuses feudal attitudes in government positions, and "fascist, racist, and xenophobe tendencies" to exclude parts of the population from social and economic life. Democratic Party of Serbia (DSS) and New Serbia (NS) The Democratic Party of Serbia of Vojislav Koštunica has been brought to life in 1992, when it split from the DS, due to disagreements about the alliance strategies, and mainly due political differences in nationalist questions. The party wanted a new drawing of the state borders according to the ethnic principle, or differently expressed it supported the Greater Serbia project, based on the idea that Serbia is everywhere where Serbians live.17 This means as well that it opposed the peace treaties of Dayton and Erdut that Slobodan Milošević agreed in, ending the war in Bosnia and Herzegovina and Croatia, not wanting to recognize the new state borders (Goati, 2004: 43). In the period of 2000 to 2007, the DSS used a much more conciliating rhetoric towards neighboring states and internal minorities. The DSS remained skeptical about cooperation with the ICTY, but its position was fairly oscillating. Kostunica, now in the position of the president of the Former Republic of Yugoslavia (2000-2003), vetoed the extradition of Slobodan Milošević, that then happened against his will, provoked a state crisis, and initiated the DSS escape from the DOS movement in 2001 (Goati, 2004: 196). While Koštunica repeatedly blamed the ICTY as an anti-Serbian institution, after taking the office of the prime minister (heading two governments in 2004-2007 and 2007-2008), he officially declared the willingness of the government for cooperation. The record has however been rather mixed, and the EU accession stalled, due to the official incapability (or rather the supposed unwillingness) to extradite the highest-ranked accused war leaders. The DSS did as well continue its clerically policy towards the Serbian Orthodox church. DSS has a tradition as a right-wing party representing the interests of an economic elite, but due to a structural change of the party electorate, the economic direction changed after 2000 (Goati, 2004: 208-209). The DSS membership before these changes could be best characterized as a nationalist intellectual and economic elite, and it did not heavily change before the democratic period after 2000, when the party became more successful in elections, and it could address a wider public. The DSS is an associate member of the European People's Party since 2005.

Serbian Radical Party (SRS) and Serbian Progress Party (SNS)

In the 1990s, the Serbian Radical Party was pushing for a more aggressive confrontation of the Serbian state and the Jugoslav army against its neighbours and against its internal minorities, not only in politics but as well on the battlefield. Party leader Vojislav Šešelj ran in parallel the paramilitary Serbian Chetnik Movement (Srpski Četnički Pokret, SČP), organising ethnic cleansing. After the end of the war and the changes of 2000, the party has not changed its goal of Greater Serbia. In 2003, Šešelj surrendered to the ICTY, accused for war crimes, while the party officials in Belgrade have rather focussed on different policy fields and tried to get more acceptable to the Serbian voters and to the international community, that continues its embargo on all contacts with SRS officials at all levels.23 The deputy party leader Tomislav Nikolić, now leading party manager, has rather tried to position the Radicals as a conservative European party, trying to imitate the metamorphosis of other formerly fascist or ultra-nationalist parties such as the National Alliance (Alleanza Nazionale, AN) in Italy, or the Croatian Democratic Movement (Hrvatska Demokratska Zajednica, HDZ), both now accepted parties on the European floor. But success of this strategy is not quite visible, either because the party is stuck deeper in the brown mire than its Croat counterpart, or because the party is commanded by its war-lord Šešelj, although now from the prison cell of the ICTY in the Netherlands. Šešelj does not only continue to be a present personality in the political debate in Serbia, through his mainly political defence in the Hague Court, and through his sporadic orders that reach his party back in Belgrade. Important events created by Šešelj were for instance his hunger strike, opening the SRS campaign for the 2007 parliamentary elections. In December 2006 Šešelj published his "political testament", advising his party to oppose the integration into EU and NATO, and to re-open territorial questions of Greater Serbia. Nikolić set an accent on social and economic issues. The party campaigned increasingly for losers of the economic transition. In the presidential electoral campaign in 2008, Nikolić as Radical candidate and other party members dropped the Šešelj badge, that they used always to wear in public, and tried to appeal to voters presenting himself with the promise of change and of to fighting against criminality and the rampant corruption in Serbia. This, however, sounds irritating, since his party is seen to stand close to the Serbian organised criminality, including to the assassinators of Đinđić (and the party is expected that it would grant an amnesty to them, if it were to get such power.

Socialist Party of Serbia (SPS)

The Socialist Party of Serbia has a long legacy, being the successor of the Union of Communists in Serbia (Savez Komunista Srbije). It re-named in 1990, but stayed under the leadership of the previous secretary of the Serbian communists, Slobodan Milošević. The party was not only the main force of the economic left in Serbia, it mainly got known in the 1990s for its authoritarian and nationalist policies. After 1991, the party started to advocate a Greater Serbia, and in the program of 1992, it called the Northern-Atlantic and European institutions, EU, OSCE, NATO, imperialist organizations and enemies of Serbia (Vykoupilová & Stojarová, 2007). The Socialists rejected any autonomy for Vojvodina and Kosovo. In the 1996 program), and the minority-friendly program points existed only on paper, but did not have an impact on the implemented policies (Goati, 2004: 50-51). With this program of international isolation, hatred, and authoritarianism the SPS' popularity dropped, and in the reasonably free and fair elections of December 2000, the party could not any more substitute popularity with electoral fraud.

The Social Democratic Party family Several parties aspire to hold the place of the Social Democratic party in Serbia. There are a few parties which are not only calling themselves Social Democrats, but also being oriented upon the Western European model of Social Democrats, with civic-liberal values and a social-redistributive program. The most important party in this field is the Social Democratic Party (Socijaldemokratska partija, SDP), which is an SI member. But these parties fall short of votes; none of these parties is able pass the electoral threshold on its own, or as the leader of a party coalition. Apart from these parties, the Social Democratic space is occupied by the DS, another SI member. Finally, several regional Vojvodina parties, the most important among them being the LSV, locate themselves in the Social Democratic realm (cf. Bochsler, 2008a). Slobodan Milosevic is accused for made   genocide against Albanians, Croats and Bosnians during the 1990s war on former territory of the former Yugoslavia.

Profiles of the main political parties in the 2010 Bosnia and Herzegovina general elections.

Party of Democratic Action (Stranka Demokratske Akcije), SDA
Leader: Sulejman Tihic

The oldest and historically the most powerful Bosniak party, the SDA was formed in 1990 by Alija Izetbegovic, the wartime President of Bosnia and Herzegovina. The current leader, Sulejman Tihic, was appointed in 2001 following the retirement through ill health of Izetbegović. Though the reputation of the SDA has declined from the glory days of the mid-1990s, and although their recent presidential candidates, Sulejman Tihic and Bakir Izetbegovic, have been unable to approach the near-universal popularity of Alija Izetbegovic, they remain a powerful force in Bosniak and Bosnian politics and the strongest party in the country's central parliament and in the parliament of its Croat-Bosniak part. Their aim in 2010 will be to regain the Bosniak seat on the country's tripartite presidency which was taken by the Party for Bosnia and Herzegovina in 2006 while retaining their hold on the central and Croat-Bosniak parliament - a tall order.

Party for Bosnia and Herzegovina, (Stranka za Bosnu i Hercegovinu),SBiH
Leader: Haris Silajdzic
Though founded in 1996, the Party for Bosnia and Herzegovina only achieved real success in the 2006 general election, when it succeeded in ousting the SDA's Sulejman Tihić from the Bosniak seat on the national presidency. Its success in 2006 was largely a result of its staunch opposition to the April 2006 constitutional reform package, which would have seen some power transferred from the entity governments to the central government.

The BiH, and its presidential candidate Haris Silajdzic, criticized the package as being too tame as it preserved a provision known as entity

voting, which allows the Bosnian Serb minority in the central parliament to veto almost anything they deem to be against the interests of the Republika Srpska. Silajdzic generally insists on greater centralization of government and limiting the power of entities - something desperately unpopular among Serbs, but popular among Bosniaks. His self-confessed long term desire is abolishment of entities. The challenge for the SBiH in 2010 will be to overtake the SDA in Bosnia-Herzegovina's central parliament and in the parliament of the Federation, while also retaining the Bosniak seat on the Presidency—success that would cement their position as the leading Bosniak party and consign the presumption of SDA rule to the history books.
Alliance of Independent Social Democrats (Savez nezavisnih socijaldemokrata-SNSD)
Leader: Milorad Dodik

The largest Serb party in Bosnia-Hercegovina, the SNSD is led by nationalist Milorad Dodik, Prime Minister of the Republika Srpska, RS, who in the 2010 election will be standing for President of the Republika Srpska. The party's is strongly oposed to any strengthening of Bosnia's central institutions and is instead calling for the return of some competencies that had been transfered from the entities to the state over the past 15 years. Dodik has repeatedly threatened with secession of the Republika Srpska from the rest of the country.

The party's breakthrough election was 2006, when it swept the board in the general elections, becoming the strongest Serb party in Bosnia-Hercegovina's central parliament and winning 41 out of 83 seats in the National Assembly of Republika Srpska. The party also took the Presidency of the Republika Srpska and the Serb seat on the tripartite Bosnian Presidency. It formed the government of the RS with Milorad Dodik as Prime Minister. Following the 2006 election the party became the largest Serb party, supplanting the Serbian Democratic Party that had been founded by Radovan Karadžić.

Social Democratic Party (Socijaldemoktratska partija Bosne i Hercegovine),SDP
Leader: Zlatko Lagumdzija

Technically the successor to the old Communist party, the SDP is one of few parties to enjoy genuinely multi-ethnic support in Bosnia, consistently polling well among Bosniaks, Croats, and others - though generally less well among Serbs.The demographics of SDP support are reflected both in the Presidency, where Zeljko Komsic has beaten the main Croat parties by virtue of his multi-ethnic support, and in the central parliament, where all of the party's five elected seats come from the Federation. The SDP is generally more focused on the economic and social issues, but it also opposes ethnic divisions and calls for a stronger, multi-ethnic state which perhaps explains its lack of popularity among Bosnia's Serbs. In 2010, its challenge will be to retain its seat on the Presidency and attempt to bolster its support among Bosniak and Croat voters for the central parliament and for the parliament of the Federation; making inroads into the Republika Srpska vote seems unlikely, though, in what will surely be a bumper year for the SNSD.

Croatian Democratic Union (Hrvatska Demokratska Zajednica BosneiHercegovine),HDZ
Leader: Dragan Covic

Historically the foremost Croat party in Bosnia, the HDZ BiH has strong links with the HDZ in Croatia. Its domination of Croat politics in Bosnia was destroyed, though, by the 2006 split that saw two factions created from the party: the HDZ-BiH on the one hand, and the HDZ-1990 on the other. Between them, they have split the previous HDZ support relatively evenly; the HDZ/BiH has three elected seats in the central parliament, and the HDZ-1990 has two. A more drastic consequence of this split support, however, has been on the presidency, where the Croat seat - previously a formality for the HDZ - has been taken by the SPD's

Zeljko Komsic. The policies of the HDZ generally centre upon the rights of Croats in a system that they view as putting the needs of Bosniaks and Serbs before the needs of Croats. As such, they propose a constitutional reform whereby a third, Croat entity would be created from what is currently the Federation, leaving the country with three distinct, ethnically based regions, each with high levels of autonomy.

The HDZ's challenge in 2010 will be first to regain their presidential seat, but second to overcome the split and re-establish themselves as the premier Croat party. However, its presidential candidate Borjana Kristo looks unlikely to trouble the SDP's Komsic.

Croatian Democratic Union 1990 (Hrvatska demokratska zajednica 1990),HDZ-1990
Leader: Bozo Ljubic
Following its split from the HDZ-BiH, the HDZ-1990 has enjoyed similar levels of success, taking 6.10 per cent of the vote in the central parliament in 2006 to the HDZ-BiH's 7.99 per cent, a balance that looks unlikelty to change significantly in 2010. Similar as HDZ's Kristo, its presidential candidate, Martin Raguž, also looks unlikely to overcome SDP's Komšić in the presidential race. The likely result in the 2010 election then, is a retention of their current position or perhaps a slight improvement; significant gains seem, at this stage, unlikely.
Serb Democratic Party (Srpska demokratska stranka), SDS
Leader: Mladen Bosic

Founded in 1992 by Radovan Karadzic, the SDS was until 2006 the most popular Serb party, enjoying near-total domination in the Republika Srpska. It has continued to enjoy significant success, despite - or perhaps because of the indictment of several of its former leading personalities, such as Radovan Karadzić and Momcilo Krajisnik, by the UN war crimes tribunal in The Hague. In 2006, however, it was overtaken as the leading Serb party by Milorad Dodik's SNSD, and there has been an uneasy rivalry between the two ever since. The SDS has been weakened by a combination of Dodik's charisma, the international sanctions and factional infighting that reached a nadir with the 2009 murder of Branislav Garić, Vice President of the SDS, by the disgruntled head of a construction company amid allegations of corruption and cronyism. In an effort to challenge SNSD dominance, the SDS has formed an opposition coalition with the third-biggest Serb party, the Party of Democratic Progress, PDP-RS, and the Serb Radical Party, SRS, called Zajedno za Srpsku. It remains to be seen, though, whether this will allow the three parties to pool their resources, or simply result in higher levels of factionalism. Given these difficulties, and given that the SNSD has gone from strength-to-strength in the past four years, the SDS's hopes for the 2010 election look bleak.

CONCLUSIONS:

- Without consolidating the market economy in the Western Balkans, and without developing a capitalist economy based on the work of companies or enterprises, there can be no political profile of the parties in this Europe.
- The formation of economic classes in the Western Balkans is the main problem of party profiling.
- The outlook of the socio-economic classes is rather sluggish in the Western Balkans, if carefully observed since political pluralism has been functioning since the 1990s, the Western Balkans can not be overcome by the dogmas of communism that have experienced the region, these consequences are still seen today, It is important that new generations of younger educated generations are coming up for the democracy and the state, and this new generation can bring about changes in the economic and social classroom.

- The Western Balkans is also strange in terms of historical developments, harder than the Balkan states neglect nationalism, and historical education in the Balkans is taught only from the hate of the Balkan peoples among themselves, this is hindering the democratization and acceptance of the reality that is political in the Balkans. History and great events over the centuries have left great consequences in the Balkan peoples also in terms of conceptualization and political profile.

- Communism in the Balkan states has contributed to the conservation of the nationalism of the Balkan peoples, the Balkan States are more concerned with regional nationalism then the economic policies and social ones.

- Even after the advent of the market economy in the Western Balkans from the former communist states, there are still many problems of feudal politics and medieval behavior, so politics still has religious connotations, but there is also a strong nationalist connotation for Balkan developments.

- The Balkan States have not passed a more natural class history because, since Balkan feudalism, a large part of the states accepted communist ideology and communism seems to have adversely affected and the consequences that are still present in the Western Balkans.

- The formation of economic classes in the peripheral Balkans are overdue, there is a politics that dominates the public proclamation of wealth, the unmanaged legal enrichment with failed privatization. Poor politicians of the state leadership, politics are the basic foundation for making private wealth , many Balkans high politicians are thrilled with economic crimes, unbiased enrichment, while these politicians are powerful enough that in their stats   control the justice system.

- So by the politics these people have benefited to make fortune and try to build economic classes and party profiles. Balkan Stats are faced with nationalism and beneficial owner of assets, so the process of establishing a political profile is difficult, but political struggle is often too harsh for due to public wealth and attempt to gain wealth. These once poor people are slowly becoming wealthy and creating an economic class. Once the creation of stable economic classes will not have a left or right political profile, there is still a war for the class, who is becoming rich and poor, so it is not known when the stability of the class will occur.

- In the Balkans, no matter what the program has or feels rightist or leftist is important to convince the citizen to vote for them, most of the political promises remain unfulfilled, promises simply are just part of a political game that requires the vote and they continue to work towards the class foundation.

- In the Balkans it often happens to change the right or left program concepts because of the easier conviction of the citizens to vote in the elections.

- Leftist ideals are more powerful in Albania and Serbia and Bosnia than in Kosovo or Montenegro. The biggest leftist and communist nostalgia in Serbia has made it a nationalist party combined with the medieval spirit while in Montenegro still seems to be a positive spirit of building right-wing politics and as well in Kosovo. In Kosovo at recent times there seem to be left-wing parties coming to strengthen due to economic uncertainty, leftist beliefs in Kosovo is growing because of social and especially health problems, perpetrators politics have pushed citizens to vote for left parties. Left and right are closer to the conservative populist right.

- It is still time for the economic class to be established and for the formation of class politics, it may happen that until 2030 there is no clear left and right policy, based on the slow development in the establishment of economic classes.

- After the establishment of economic classes in the Balkans, there will be a need for a stable, depoliticized and politically undeclared judiciary and prosecution. In this period there will be the strengthening of law and order, as well as the representation of many powerful politicians or these people will become powerful and will preserve their influence on the control of the justice authorities that will continue a period of time in order to strengthen law and order. It is not surprise the cases that today in the Balkan countries there is no major economic investment from European or large states due to the weakness and ineffectiveness of functioning justice bodies without affecting policies.

- The political party in the Western Balkans still has "doubts" whether they should be left or right, so it is too early to say whether there will be a right-wing or half-left and poor left-wing Balkans. Still, the Balkans are facing a nationalist leftist or right-wing nationalism, nationalist currents are still almost unsuitable for economic development.

- For the Balkans, the history of the Balkan peoples is more powerful than the regional development aspect, although the only hope of the Balkans is to become part of the European Union.

- Balkan political parties need to integrate with European political developments, so they must be part of the left or the right wing of Europe, leftists and rightists have their own rules in Europe to be part of, and therefore have to meet certain criteria to be part of the developments European politics. The Balkan parties must be left out of nationalism, without it being impossible to integrate into the European political scene, without it being overlooked by nationalist ideology. This is why they have lagged behind developments. Balkan nationalism hindrance completely obstructs the normality of developments, Serbia still lacks for the

Balkans and the state with a great nationalist influence, Serbia is not giving up on Russia and this seems to be the biggest concern in the Balkans.

Balkan states need to give up the war on land, which is the only problem that promotes nationalism in the Balkans. Aside from this policy, absurdities can not be integrated into European political developments in the Balkans.

LITERATURE

Blerim Burjani, Electoral Reform,2014

Blerim Burjani, International Crises, 2010

PDK Statute

Political Program of PDK

LDK Statute

LDK Political Program

VV short Political Program

AAK statue and Political Program

Democratic Party of Albania

Key Political Parties in Albania, http://www.balkaninsight.com/en/article/who-is-who-political-parties-in-albania,21.05.2018

Socialist Political Party of Albania

Socialist Party for Integration

Partia per Bashkim Demokratik

Montenegro Kay Political Parties   http:// www. balkaninsight. com/en/ article /montenegro-key-political-parties

Political Parties in Serbia, https://www.bochsler.eu/publi/bochsler_serbiacountry.pdf
https://www.bochsler.eu/publi/bochsler_serbiacountry.pdf, 24.05.2018

Printed by Books on Demand GmbH, Norderstedt / Germany